Reading and Writing Poetry Across the Year

Georgia Heard
Lester Laminack

*first*hand

An imprint of Heinemann
361 Hanover Street
Portsmouth, NH 03801-3912
www.firsthand.heinemann.com

Offices and agents throughout the world

Climb Inside a Poem, Original Poems for Children
ISBN-10: 0-325-01721-2 ISBN-13: 978-0-325-01721-1

Lessons for Climb Inside a Poem
ISBN-10: 0-325-01722-0 ISBN-13: 978-0-325-01722-8

Reading and Writing Poetry Across the Year
ISBN-10: 0-325-01723-9 ISBN-13: 978-0-325-01723-5

Climb Inside a Poem full set
ISBN-10: 0-325-00983-X ISBN-13: 978-0-325-00983-4

Library of Congress Cataloging-in-Publication Data on file at the Library of Congress.

Printed in the United States of America on acid-free paper

11 10 09 08 07 VP 1 2 3 4 5

To my son Leo who teaches me to see the world with wonder.

—G.H.

To my son Zachary who sees beauty in all creation.

—L.L.L.

Acknowledgments

The collaboration on this project began in a bookstore. It grew out of our responses to the small amount of poetry this particular bookstore made available for children. As we talked, our conversation moved to brainstorming, and like a trickle becomes a river pouring into the gulf, our ideas rushed forward, merging into a healthy flow. We shared our thinking with Lois Bridges, who believed in the need for making poetry readily available for teachers and children in ways that could be part of the daily routine across the year. We are grateful to her for that faith and advocacy. As the project evolved, Kate Montgomery, our editor, guided us through the rough spots and nudged us to see new possibilities. We are grateful, Kate, for your wisdom tempered with your kind and gentle guidance. Many thanks to Amy Gilbert, who worked tirelessly behind the scenes making sure all the loose ends were tied together. This project, of course, hinges on the poetry involved, and we are indebted both to the poets who shared their talents and insights and to Terri Murphy for adding inspiration and art.

from Lester:

Climb Inside a Poem grew beyond our initial vision and took more time than any of us imagined it might. I am most grateful to Georgia, who picked up the challenge with grace and wisdom. My thanks to my family and my dearest friend Reba for your undying support through a trying year, and finally to Steve. You bring out the best in me.

from Georgia:

It takes a village to create a book, and I'm grateful to so many people for their inspiration and support. Thank you, Lester, for sparking the fire that became *Climb Inside a Poem*. Thank you to Jane Hig for your wise teaching and treasured morning talks, and to the teachers at the Benjamin School. Also, thanks to the American School of London for further inspiration. And finally to my family: Dermot, for your love, and Leo, for the wonder of it all.

In addition, we'd like to acknowledge all of the students over the years, some with whom we've lost touch, whose beautiful poetry has stayed with us.

Table of Contents

INTRODUCTION to *Reading and Writing Poetry Across the Year*

Children are natural poets. They speak poetry all day long. Every day, they say wonderful little poetic gems that surprise and delight us and help us look at the world in a new way. A few years ago when my son was five, he drew a picture and said, "Mom, here's my poem!" Pointing to his drawing, he recited: "I sleep in the night. The moon is on my face. I float up to space as the angels carry me to the moon and stars. The road, my bed, the house are floating floating floating up to the moon and stars."

My son was doing what a lot of young poets do: imagining their poems in their minds first, and then speaking their poems out loud. My son is a typical, ordinary, wonderful genius of a child who also has a poetic sensibility. The truth is that all children have a poetic sensibility. They are all natural poets.

Children and poets share a similar way of looking at the world. Children and poets both:

- Discover importance in small moments
- Find wonder in the ordinary
- See beauty even in ugliness
- Burst with curiosity
- Enjoy the sounds of words
- Look at life in a unique way
- Create their own language to describe the world
- Feel their feelings with great force

Given children's natural affinity for poetry, we believe that poetry should be woven throughout the whole school year in the elementary grades. If we wait until National Poetry Month in April, we've missed many opportunities to build on our students' natural poetic abilities! In addition, reading and writing poetry can support and extend young children's language and literacy development in many ways.

Reading poetry can help children:

- **Connect personally to their texts.** Poetry is personal, and it can connect children to reading through listening to and reading poems about their own lives.
- **Feel successful as a reader.** Children can read some poetry more easily than stories because many poems are relatively short. Often, children will hear a poem more than once, become familiar with the words, catch on to the rhythm or rhyme, and be able to read the poem back with less effort than they could a different type of text. When children feel that they can successfully read a poem, they become more confident readers.
- **Develop fluency.** Poetry is written to be read with special attention to rhythm, cadence, and pacing—all of which are essential to fluency in reading.
- **Develop word awareness.** Children are delighted with the play of words in poetry, particularly with the use of unusual and surprising words. Language play, rhyme, and repetition help create a pattern in young readers' minds. The pattern is like a handle that allows them to carry the poem away after reading or listening. The lingering memories of the poem will trigger word play in their speaking and writing.
- **Support basic concepts of print.** Poems can be used to teach and reinforce print concepts such as left-to-right progression of text, spaces between words, letter and sound correspondence, and punctuation.
- **Deepen the reading-writing connection.** Children will be reading their own poems in class shares and to peers, which will reinforce reading skills.

Writing poetry can help children:

- **Make a personal connection to writing.** Poetry is often personal, and it embraces many topics and forms, which will give children the freedom and inspiration to write what really matters to them.
- **Write with feeling and voice.** Poetry is often experiential and emotional, so children learn to express their own experiences—with feeling and an authentic voice.
- **Feel successful as a writer.** Poems are often short, so children can write a complete poem in a few lines and feel they have created a successful piece of writing. Success brings comfort and pride, and as children grow in comfort, they gain confidence to attempt more complex tasks as readers and writers.
- **Write about particulars.** Poetry is often quite focused. It zeros in on the essence of a subject and teaches children how to find significance in the small and the ordinary.

- **Learn to love words.** Children love the surprising and the unusual, the new and the energetic. When we draw attention to the language of poetry, they will consume it like the essential nutrient it is.

An Overview of *Climb Inside a Poem: Reading and Writing Poetry Across the Year*

There are three parts of this set:

- *Climb Inside a Poem* big book
- *Lessons for Climb Inside a Poem*
- *Reading and Writing Poetry Across the Year*

What Is in *Climb Inside a Poem*?

In the big book, you will find 29 original poems written by some of our very favorite children's poets. We've commissioned the wonderful illustrator Terri Murphy to illustrate each poem in ways that we know will scaffold children's ability to read and understand each poem. We've loosely arranged the poems so that the easier ones are toward the beginning of the book and the more complex ones are nearer to the end. We've also tried, in some cases, to cluster them together by theme so that reading them in sequence will provoke intertextual thoughts in readers or listeners.

What Is in *Lessons for Climb Inside a Poem*?

In this book of lessons, you'll find suggestions for ways to work with every poem in the big book for 5 to 10 minutes per day over the course of one week. We have presented ideas for working with each poem from Monday through Friday. On Mondays, the activity ideas are meant to help introduce the poem to children; on Tuesdays and Wednesdays, the activity ideas are meant to support children in exploring the poem in more depth; on Thursdays, we offer information to help children get to know the poet and the poet's body of work; and on Fridays, the activities are designed to help children focus on the poet's crafting moves. At the end of the lesson book, in the "Poet Profiles" section, you'll find more about our featured poets, including photographs, biographical information, and some "poet-to-poet" advice they offer for our young poets.

What Is in *Reading and Writing Poetry Across the Year*?

In the *Reading and Writing Poetry Across the Year* guidebook, we offer a range of minilessons and activity suggestions for reading and writing time over the course of the year.

In "Part One: Creating a Poetry-Rich Environment," we offer suggestions for setting up the classroom in ways that make the study of poetry easy, fun, and fruitful. In this section, you'll find suggestions for setting up different kinds of poetry centers, ideas for bulletin boards that feature poetry, and suggestions for other environmental structures to support children in engaging with poems.

In "Part Two: Reading Poetry," we offer a dozen minilessons that you can use to help children enrich their understandings of poems you read to them, and to help them learn to become strong readers of poetry themselves.

In "Part Three: Writing Poetry," we provide a complete poetry writing unit of study. Over the course of the unit, you will help children find inspiration, try new poetic forms, revise and edit their writing, and celebrate their poems. At key points, you'll find suggestions for ways to work with children individually on predictable problems, and ways to help them assess and grow stronger in their poetry work.

Using the Three Parts of the *Climb Inside a Poem* Set

What is the best way to weave in poetry throughout the year in the elementary grades? Waiting until April for National Poetry Month is too late to introduce poetry, but given our curricular needs and packed schedules, is it possible to make a place for poetry throughout the year? After years of practice in the classroom, we can tell you that it's not only possible but *vital* to weave poetry into the daily fabric of a school day by reading a variety of poems for a variety of purposes throughout the year.

Plan Short, Daily Poetry Experiences from September to June

The first thing we must plan is to read a poem aloud every single day, Monday through Friday, at a predictable time—first thing in the morning, the last few minutes at the end of the day, after lunch or recess, during transition times—any of these times or any other could work. My preference is to start every day with a poem because it sets a calm tone and sets up the morning language arts block. It only takes a few minutes to read a poem. Have fun, and introduce children to a wide range of poems: silly, hysterical, quiet, serious, reflective, rhythmic, free-verse, and so on. You can use the poems in the *Climb Inside a Poem* big book. Then, turn to the corresponding suggestions from the *Lessons for Climb Inside a Poem* book. Using just those two books, you can offer your youngsters a short poetry experience every day, all year long.

Plan a Few Longer, Deeper Poetry Experiences to Punctuate the Year

Over the course of the year, though children will have 5 to 10 minutes of poetry every day, they will need other experiences that give them a chance to appreciate poetry in greater depth.

Poetry in Fall: "Creating a Poetry-Rich Environment"

When you are ready to deepen children's experience with poetry, return to this guidebook, *Reading and Writing Poetry Across the Year*. Start with "Part One: Creating a Poetry-Rich Environment," and select some suggestions and activities for immersing young children in poetry. Set up ways for your youngsters to bathe in poetry, splash in it, and drink it in thirstily! Without feeling what it is like to be immersed in poetry, without the essence of poetry all around them, it will be difficult for them to engage in meaningful reading or writing of poems.

In the first section of "Part Two: Reading Poetry," you will find more suggestions that will help you immerse children in the rhythm and sense of verse. These minilessons, too, will be useful to you early in the year.

Poetry in Winter: "Reading Poetry"

Once your children have become accustomed to poetry through immersion and lots of reading of poems, you will be ready to lead them in reading poetry even more deeply. The minilessons in "Part Two: Reading Poetry" will help you do that—children will hear more poems throughout the course of the day, and they'll learn ways to support their own budding understandings of poems through reading them with special attention to what makes poetry, poetry. You might plan to use these minilessons once or twice per week over the course of the winter. We've presented these minilessons from most simple to most complex, but this sequence is highly flexible, and you should pick and choose the lessons that are right for your children at any given time.

Poetry in Spring: "Writing Poetry"

In the springtime, once children have been immersed in poetry for several months and have read poetry for several months, they will be bursting to write their own poems. Now is the time to turn to "Part Three: Writing Poetry," and use the minilessons you find there to launch the poetry writing unit of study that will take the place of other writing time for 3 to 4 weeks. Unlike "Part Two: Reading Poetry," the minilessons in this section are a cohesive unit; they are meant to be used in the sequence in which they are presented, each lesson directly following the other, with no other writing lessons interspersed.

All these plans aside, the poems and activities in these three books are meant to support and inspire you and your children to climb inside poetry. The individual, unique ways you invent to do so—the ways that sprout from your interests, your passions, and your experiences—will be far more organic and tailored to your wonderful, special students than anything we can offer you. We invite you to enjoy what we present here and, with your children, to make much, much more of it!

Creating a Poetry-Rich Environment

Creating a Poetry-Rich Environment

From the first day of school, we can create a classroom environment that will nurture a love of poetry in children—a love that can last them their whole lives. By setting up a poetry-rich environment, we can offer young learners the opportunity to explore poetry, piquing their curiosity before poetry becomes an official topic of study. Poetry exploration activities and poetry centers support reading and writing habits helpful to all genres of writing, and most of all, they begin to reveal to children the power of poetry.

The *Climb Inside a Poem* big book provides a starter set of sample poems so you can have wonderful examples of poems at your fingertips to read aloud and display around the room even on the first day of school. Many of the lessons in the program include a list of Book Links so you can extend your lesson with more examples. There is also a bibliography of excellent collections of poems at the back of this book, and you will undoubtedly add many of your own favorite poems!

The following lessons are ways to help you make poetry part of the daily life of your class. Select and try out any of the following suggestions and activities for immersing young children in poetry. These poetry exploration activities and poetry center possibilities are meant to help you bring poetry into the minds of children through watching, listening, feeling, reading, and writing. You'll notice many of the minilessons are designed to help children focus on noticing poetry in the world around us—in our speech, in picture books, and in special words and phrases. Other minilessons are designed to help children find inspiration for writing poetry. The more of these minilessons you try with your students, the more they (and you) will fall in love with poetry and be eager to begin writing poems!

Noticing Poetry in What We Say

Sometimes kids talk poetry to each other without knowing it. —Deborah Chandra

Once when I asked a kindergartner what a poet is, she replied, "A poet is something that swims in water." What struck me was the pure poetry of her reply, despite the fact that she wasn't able to define "poet"! Children speak poetry all day long—wonderful little poetic gems, like the one above, that surprise and delight us and help us look at the world in a new way.

Even before you introduce poetry formally, listen to your students talk and find the seeds of poems in their natural, everyday language. This doesn't mean listening for words that rhyme but, instead, listening for words that feel true, expressions that surprise us, or language that describes something in a new or beautiful way. Collect these overheard lines of poetry in a notebook or file.

Once you have collected several examples, create a bulletin board entitled "What We Say Is Poetry" where you can post them. Keep listening throughout the days for spoken poems or "seeds" of poems. Have paper strips handy so you, and eventually your students also, can easily write down these "seeds" and post them on the board. Be sure to reserve time at least once a week to read the spoken poems that have been "caught" throughout the week. Stop the class periodically during the day for everyone to listen to a "caught" poem. You can keep adding to the "What We Say Is Poetry" board throughout the year. Poetry will be sprouting everywhere once children recognize the poetry in their everyday words!

Minilesson

I've been listening to your words every day, and what I'm noticing is that you are speaking poetry all day long! Sometimes you'll use a wonderful word, and I'll just want to stop you because the word is so interesting. Or you'll describe something in an unusual way, and I'll want to say to you, "That could be the seed of a poem!" I think we need to collect and appreciate these seeds of poems, so I've made a special place on the bulletin board called "What We Say Is Poetry." Whenever I hear you say a poetic word or speak poetry, I'm going to ask you to write down your spoken poem on one of these strips to display on the board! That will help us remember that we speak poetry here all the time.

Every week we'll share our spoken poems aloud. Here, let me read from the board some of what I've heard so far from you. [Teachers, you'll want to insert your own overheard poems at this point.]

"My leg is screaming pain!" *(spoken when Emily came into the classroom after knocking her leg against a bench in the hallway)*

"My family is like a cloud of best friends." *(spoken during morning circle by a first-grade poet, Sakou)*

"The sky was opening and the sun was closing and the grass was turning back and forth." *(spoken by Jacob after taking a class walk outside)*

Noticing Poetry in What We Read

I love finding the right words. The stupendous, the magnificent, and the ordinary words. I collect them. . . .
—Rebecca Kai Dotlich

Poetry can be found almost anywhere—not just in poetry books. Create a bulletin board entitled "Amazing Words," where you can post examples of true, amazing, beautiful, interesting, vivid words and sentences selected from stories and other read alouds. Highlight examples of poetic language in your read alouds throughout the day, and write down these phrases to post.

Minilesson

When I'm reading aloud to you, or when you're reading during independent reading time, if you hear or read a word or a line that is beautiful, vivid, unusual, or poetic, I hope you stop and write it down in your notebooks or share it with the class. We can celebrate words—words we love, words that are unusual, words that surprise us, words that make powerful images, and words that make us think of our own memories—by writing them down and posting them on our "Amazing Words" board.

Let me read some examples of "Amazing Words" from a bulletin board in a class I know well. Children found these lines in the picture book *Night in the Country* by Cynthia Rylant. Listen: "Great owls with marble eyes who swoop among the trees . . ." and "Night frogs who sing songs for you every night. . . ."

Children found these poetic lines in Ralph Fletcher's beautiful picture book *Twilight Comes Twice*:

"With invisible arms
dawn erases the stars from the blackboard of night . . ."

And children picked this word from the title of a Kevin Henke's book because they loved the sound of it: "chrysanthemum." What a great word! Let's all say it out loud together and feel the music of that word in our mouths.

When we linger over poetic words and lines, we begin to notice that powerful and poetic language can be found everywhere—not just in poems!

Book Links

Here are a few picture books that are wonderfully poetic:

Cynthia Rylant
Night in the Country
Atheneum/Richard Jackson Books (1986)

Ralph Fletcher
Twilight Comes Twice
Clarion Books (1997)

Ralph Fletcher
Hello, Harvest Moon
Clarion Books (2003)

Lester Laminack
Saturdays and Teacakes
Peachtree Publishers (2004)

Tony Johnston
The Barn Owls
Charlesbridge Publishing (2000)

Sheree Fitch
No Two Snowflakes
Orca Book Publishers (2001)

Rebecca Kai Dotlich
What Is Science?
Henry Holt and Co. (2006)

Jane Yolen
Owl Moon
Philomel (1987)

Eileen Spinelli
When Mama Comes Home Tonight
Simon & Schuster (1998)

Mem Fox
Koala Lou
Voyager Books (1994)

Joanne Ryder
My Mother's Voice
HarperCollins (2006)

Elisha Cooper
Beach
Orchard Books (2006)

Nikki Grimes
Welcome, Precious
Orchard Books (2006)

Irene Kelly
It's a Butterfly's Life
Holiday House (2007)

Collecting Amazing Words

Get acquainted with lots of words; they are your tools. Have fun with their sounds—turn them round on your tongue, feel them bump and hiss and slip, and notice how different speech sounds make you feel. —Deborah Chandra

Poets and writers love the sounds of words. This is very true for children as well. You can set up word-play areas so that when students have a little extra time—such as in the morning when they first come into school or during center time—they can have fun playing with words. This will serve them well when they begin to write poetry, and it will strengthen their word skills for all their writing.

Minilesson

I want to read to you what the writer Roald Dahl wrote in his notebook: "When I began my career as a writer, I started collecting words in an old school notebook. Keeping lists [of words] which I can easily refer to when I'm writing helps me to find the exact word I'm looking for."

Writers and poets collect wonderful words to use in stories and poems. We've started a class collection of wonderful words on our "Amazing Words" board, and now you're going to be starting your very own collection of wonderful words. I'm giving each of you a metal ring and some blank cards that you can attach to it to make a word ring. When you think of or read a word that you absolutely love—either because of its sound or its meaning—you can write it on a card and put it on your word ring. You can keep this word ring on your desk and you'll have wonderful word possibilities at your fingertips while you're writing.

Here are examples of wonderful words that Becca, a second grader, collected: *peeked*, *whispered*, *swiftly*, *scurried*, *crackle*, *sizzled*, *glided*, and *dangling*.

Book Links

These books can help you extend the minilesson.

Roni Schotter
The Boy Who Loved Words
Random House (2006)

Ann and Paul Rand
Sparkle and Spin: A Book About Words
Chronicle Books (2006)

Playing with Rhyming Words

One way to bring rhymes into the classroom environment is to set up an ongoing rhyming activity. You might say something like, "Let's play a game with rhyming words! I'll write a word at the top of this chart paper, and your job is to write down every rhyme you can for that word. Let's try it. Hmm. I'll start with the word *cat*, and I'll write it here at the top. What words rhyme with *cat*? During the day, whenever you can think of a word that rhymes with *cat*, just write it down right here. In a couple of days, we'll see how many rhyming words you've found."

To make sure you choose words that will lend themselves to this activity, you could look in a rhyming dictionary or on the website www.rhymer.com for words with many rhymes. Thinking about commonly found word endings (*-ay*, *-at*, *-ack*) might also ensure long, fun-filled lists!

You might want to share this interesting fact with your students: there are some words in the English language that have no rhymes. For example, the words *orange*, *wolf*, *purple*, *month*, and *silver* have no real rhymes. There are what we call "slant" rhymes to go with these words, which are not true rhymes, such as for *wolf*: *gulf*, *fur*, *enough*.

I've given the following minilesson to kindergarten children using the poem "Song for My Swing" by Patricia Hubbell (p. 19 in the *Climb Inside a Poem* big book). Be sure to read the poem all the way through first, and then play this fun rhyming game. Display the poem with the following rhyming words covered: *sky*, *pass*, *hair*, *place*. Write those words on a separate chart in a different order from that in which they appear in the poem.

Minilesson

Today I'm going to read to you a poem by Patricia Hubbell called "Song for My Swing," and then we're going to play a little rhyming game. I've covered up the rhyming words, and I'd like you to say what you think they might be. Here are the rhyming words that I've taken out that you can choose from: *pass, place, sky, hair*. (They are not in order.)

Book Links

The following poems (among others) in the *Climb Inside a Poem* big book use rhyme:

"How I Hopscotch" by Kristine O'Connell George p. 13

"Making Soup" by Marilyn Singer p. 12

"Why? Why? Why?" by Lee Bennett Hopkins p. 9

"Where Do I Find Poetry?" by Georgia Heard p. 2

"Who's Coming to Tea?" by Jane Yolen p. 10

"Tooth Truth" by Lee Bennett Hopkins p. 7

"When I Ride My Bike" by Patricia Hubbell p. 14

"School Bus Lady" by J. Patrick Lewis p. 15

"Best Friend" by Marilyn Singer p. 17

Other texts that use rhyme:

Diane Adams
Zoom!
Peachtree (2005)

Mrya Cohn Livingston
Calendar
Holiday House (2007)

J. Patrick Lewis
Big Is Big (and little, little): A Book of Contrasts
Holiday House (2007)

Douglas Florian
Lizards, Frogs, and Polliwogs
Harcourt (2001)

Clyde Watson
Father Fox's Pennyrhymes
HarperCollins (2001)

Jack Prelutsky
Read-Aloud Rhymes for the Very Young
Knopf (1986)

Margot C. Griego, Betsy L. Bucks, Sharon S. Gilbert, Laurel H. Kimball
Tortillas Para Mamá: And Other Nursery Rhymes/Spanish and English
Henry Holt and Co. (1981)

Lissa Rovetch
Ook the Book: And Other Silly Rhymes
Chronicle Books (2001)

Rebecca Kai Dotlich
Over in the Pink House: New Jump-Rope Rhymes
Boyds Mills Press (2004)

Alice Schertle
1, 2, I Love You
Chronicle Books (2004)

5

Playing with Alliterative Words

What child doesn't love tongue twisters? When I was a girl, I repeated "She sells seashells by the seashore" over and over again, faster and faster, until it drove my parents crazy. Tongue twisters use alliteration, which is another fun, musical tool in poetry where poets repeat initial consonant sounds. Children love to invent their own alliterations, and as they're playing with alliterative words, they're becoming more aware of the sounds of language.

Minilesson

Do you know what the poet Deborah Chandra said about words? She said, "Have fun with their sounds—turn them round on your tongue, feel them bump and hiss and slip." Well, there is one thing that writers and poets sometimes do with words to make them bump or hiss, and it's called *alliteration*. That's a fancy word for repeating beginning consonant sounds. Consonants aren't vowels—they have sounds like /k/ as in *kite*, or /s/ as in *snake*. An example of alliteration is: A cute cat curls and cuddles on a cozy quilt. Do you hear the same sound at the beginning of all those words? That's *alliteration*. Poets use alliteration to create different effects in the sound of their poems. For example, using /b/ words might create a bumping sensation. Using /s/ words might create a hissing sensation.

Our Word Play Center this week is about alliteration. I'm going to write a consonant on this chart, and your job is to write down as many words as you can think of that start with that same consonant sound. This week's sound is /s/. I'm going to write it here, and during the day I'd like you to write down as many words as you can think of that start with that /s/ sound. When we've filled the chart, maybe we can write a poem from all our alliterative words! I wonder what kind of a sound and what kind of a feeling all those /s/ sounds together will make, and I wonder what we'll decide the poem should be about to match that feeling!

Book Links

These books can help you extend the minilesson.

Pamela Duncan Edwards
Some Smug Slug
HarperCollins (1996)

Uri Shulevitz
Snow
Farrar, Straus and Giroux (1998)

Reeve Lindbergh
The Awful Aardvarks Go to School
Viking Juvenile (1997)

Beverly McLoughland
A Hippo's a Heap: And Other Animal Poems
Boyds Mills Press (1993)

Valorie Fisher
Ellsworth's Extraordinary Electric Ears and Other Amazing Alphabet Anecdotes
Atheneum (2003)

Karla Kuskin
Roar and More
Boyds Mills Press (2004)

Margaret Wise Brown
Four Fur Feet
Hyperion (1994)

Sharing Favorite Poems

Read poems. Lots of poems. All kinds of poems. . . .
You'll find it becomes easier to write poems yourself.

—X. J. Kennedy

This idea of sharing favorite poems through a "poe-tree" bulletin board came from my son's wonderful second-grade teacher, Mrs. Hig, who loves poetry and simply can't wait until Poetry Month in April to share her enthusiasm for poetry. Every Thursday, each of her second-grade poets shares a favorite poem with the class that they've written or found in a book at home.

Mrs. Hig explains in a letter she sent home to parents:

> "These little poems don't have to rhyme but should be just little thoughts written in poetry form. We don't worry about correct spelling, the paper they are writing on, or pretty printing but are more concerned about the little thoughts that are within the poems. Make sure your child practices reading the poem at home. It does not have to be memorized. If they are inspired, an illustration would be nice to add."

At the beginning of Thursday's reading workshop time, a few children read their chosen poems out loud and all of the poems are displayed on a bulletin board with a paper collage of a great, leafy "poe-tree." Among many poems displayed on the board is one my son brought in, "The Octopus" by Ogden Nash:

> Tell me, O Octopus, I begs,
> Is those things arms, or is they legs?

Another child, Caroline, wrote a lovely poem and placed it on the "poe-tree":

> Love is like a song.
> Love is like a song.
> Like a heart with an arrow.
> Love is a hug or a smile.
> Like a bright star.
> Love is a story with a happy ending!

The beauty of creating this sort of a bulletin board is in honoring children's poetry choices—in honoring what they write or find. As a result, children feel the freedom of poetry possibilities.

Minilesson

Every Thursday morning for the whole school year, we're going to have a very special reading time. We're going to be reading poems: poems that you feel inspired to write and poems that you've read in a book that you'd like to share with the class. Each poem that you share will then go up on our "poe-tree" board. Just think: in one month, our tree will be covered with poems! So, start thinking about a favorite poem you'd like to share or a poem that you'd like to write to share on poetry Thursdays!

Book Links

These books can help you extend the minilesson.

Eloise Greenfield
Honey, I Love and Other Love Poems
HarperTrophy (1986)

Paul Janeczko
The Place My Words Are Looking For: What Poets Say About and Through Their Work
Simon & Schuster (1990)

Langston Hughes
The Dream Keeper and Other Poems
Knopf (1996)

Jack Prelutsky
The 20th Century Children's Poetry Treasury
Knopf (1999)

Walter Dean Myers
Brown Angels: An Album of Pictures and Verse
HarperCollins (1993)

X. J. Kennedy and Dorothy Kennedy
Talking Like the Rain: A Read-to-Me Book of Poems
Little, Brown (1992)

Finding Inspiration Through a Window

I usually write at the kitchen table, where I sit facing the living room window. When I look up from my writing I can see the woods, which relaxes my eyes and my mind.

—Beverly McLoughland

Many poems are written from close observation of the world. If you create an "Observation Window" in your classroom, you provide an added opportunity for students to look at their world carefully and write about what they see or hear. Perhaps your classroom offers a view of a city skyline or an apartment building, or maybe it's a tree or a parking lot. No matter what the view, students can practice honing their observation skills, which will benefit their writing in any genre.

To begin, outline part of a classroom window with crepe paper, colored tape, or some other material. Nearby, display finished poems that have come from close observation of the world—particularly poems about the same kinds of things your students can see through their classroom window—it might be sky, trees, pavement, or even cars. Display examples of *list poems*, which are the easiest type of poems for kids to write, and invite children to write their own list poems.

Have clipboards and poetry paper (paper cut lengthwise to suggest the shape of a poem) at the window, ready for students to write their own observations and poems. You might want to write, "I See . . . I Hear . . ." at the top of a piece of chart paper to keep at the poetry window so that kids can draw or write a list of some of what they see out the window, or they can focus on what they hear. Some kindergarten and first-grade teachers place an easel by the window, equipped with chart paper and a marker attached with a string, so that children can draw what they see and then write a few words.

Minilesson

Today we're going to start a new poetry center in the classroom, called an Observation Window. A lot of writers and poets observe the world around them to get ideas for writing. We can observe the world outside our window and write about what we notice.

Let me read you a poem written by Rebecca Kai Dotlich about looking out a window. As I read "Watching at the Window," listen carefully for all the wonderful things she observes.

Watching at the Window

By Rebecca Kai Dotlich

A corner of cloud
settles between skyscrapers,
a seagull rests
at the tip of a roof,
a yellow taxi *swooshes* by,
cars stop, then go,
a bicycle splashes
through the rain.
Puddles dot
the tops of shoes,
garbage cans,
cracked walks.
Umbrellas cuddle in twos,
a school bus sputters
at the corner,
a crossing guard
swirls a sign,
sips hot coffee,
waves while
a pair of squirrels
hunt for treasure
at the root of the tree;
a blue bit of paper
hugs the street sign,
a puppy tugs
at his leash, and . . .
the swing swings,
the wind teases
the telephone wire,
and a butterfly sails,
then settles
at the window . . .

Turn to the person next to you, and tell each other what you remember the speaker in Rebecca Kai Dotlich's poem noticed out her window.

I'm going to tape this poem right here near our window for inspiration, and I'm leaving this poetry paper and a few clipboards here so you can write your own observational poems from what you see out the window.

Book Links

Other observation-based books:

Patricia Hubbell
City Kids: Poems
Marshall Cavendish Corporation (2001)

Kristine O'Connell George
Old Elm Speaks: Tree Poems
Clarion Books (1998)

Harry Behn
Trees
Bill Martin Books (1992)

Bobbi Katz
Once Around the Sun
Harcourt (2006)

Joseph Bruchac and Jonathan London
Thirteen Moons on Turtle's Back: A Native American Year of Moons
Philomel (1992)

Jane Yolen
Bird Watch
Philomel (1990)

Finding Inspiration from Natural Objects

Sycamore leaves, spiders, lost teeth, the moon—all common objects of the world, and hiding places for something more. —Deborah Chandra

Poetry pays attention to the world. . . . It can make us stop and wonder. —Beverly McLoughland

Poets are like natural scientists in their tendency to explore their world. Many poems are sparked by observations of small, fascinating things in nature. By creating a Poetry Museum, we can help students become close observers of small, ordinary, and fascinating objects from nature that can spark their writing.

Bring in a few fascinating objects such as nests, shells, or plants, and invite children to bring in other objects from nature. Display this collection on a shelf or a table as a Poetry Museum. Hang up poems that have natural objects as their subject, especially poems about the same objects that are in your Poetry Museum. Read these poems as you show your students the objects. You can place an observation journal nearby for your students to record what they notice, and provide poetry paper to encourage them to write observation poems of their own.

Minilesson

When the poet Patricia Hubbell was a girl, she created a Poetry Museum that inspired her to write poetry. This is what she says:

> "When I was ten years old, I started a museum in the playhouse in our backyard. I filled the shelves with birds' nests, rocks, shells, pressed wildflowers, and other treasures. I spent long hours in the woods and fields collecting things. I took long walks and kept my eyes eagerly open.
>
> One day, I found a snakeskin, complete from head to tail. The thin papery skin was beautiful. I put it on a shelf where the sun would shine through it.
>
> About the time I started the museum, I began to write poems. I wrote about the sun and the rain, about riding my pony, about swimming in the ocean. I wrote about the things in my museum. Birds' nests and rocks, leaves and butterflies found their way into the poems."

Wow! A Poetry Museum! We can set up our own Poetry Museum in our classroom that might inspire us to write poems too.

I asked you last week to bring in a fascinating object from nature. We'll display these on this table to make our own museum. I'll put some poetry paper here and a few clipboards so when you feel inspired you can come to the museum and observe and write.

Book Links

The following poem in the *Climb Inside a Poem* big book is from close observation of nature:

"Spring Riddles" by Beverly McLoughland p. 29

Other observation-based texts:

Yvonne Winer
Birds Build Nests
Charlesbridge Publishing (2002)

Eileen Spinelli
Feathers: Poems About Birds
Henry Holt and Co. (2004)

Lee Bennett Hopkins
Flit, Flutter, Fly!: Poems About Bugs and Other Crawly Creatures
Doubleday (1992)

Lee Bennett Hopkins
Spectacular Science: A Book of Poems
Simon & Schuster (1999)

Douglas Florian
Handsprings
Greenwillow (2006)

Georgia Heard
Creatures of Earth, Sea, and Sky: Poems
Boyds Mills Press (1992)

Paul Paolilli and Dan Brewer
Silver Seeds: A Book of Nature Poems
Viking Juvenile (2001)

Shelley Rotner and Richard Olivo
Close, Closer, Closest
Atheneum (1997)

Valerie Worth
All the Small Poems and Fourteen More
Farrar, Straus and Giroux (1994)

Finding Inspiration on a Walk

Pay attention to the world around you—little things, big things, people, animals, buildings, events, etc. What do you see, hear, taste, smell, feel? —Marilyn Singer

To help me write, I often take walks. —Marilyn Singer

Most young children study the world, and in their seeing they help us see things we have never seen before. This is also a poet's job—to observe carefully and then to find words to express what we see.

Taking children on poetry walks will help nurture their natural habit of observing the small things all around them. You can take your students on a poetry walk on a particularly beautiful day or at a scheduled time, such as every Friday morning or every Monday after lunch. The more children are able to notice and store in their minds, the more alive and vivid their observations and poems will be. When you return to the classroom from the walk, you might want to write a shared poem first. To do this, ask students to tell you what they noticed and observed and stored in their minds from their walk outside. On chart paper, make a two-column chart. In the first column, write down what children observed. Next, create a shared poem from their observations. Here is an example:

Creating a Shared Poem from Observations on a Poetry Walk

Observations	*Poem*
The leaves were moving.	Leaves moving.
Tree trunks were standing still.	Trees standing still.
Grass was squishy.	Grass squishy.
Clouds were floating.	Clouds floating overhead.

Eventually, children will be able to write their own independent poems after these walks.

Minilesson

Today, and every Monday morning, we're going to go for a short poetry walk. On this walk, we'll have to be very quiet so we can notice everything around us and then store what we notice in our minds, and even write down in our notebooks some of the fascinating things we observe. You can listen carefully, or just watch with your eyes, or both! When we return to the classroom, we'll gather all our observations on a chart and create a poem. Okay, everybody, let's go on a poetry walk!

Book Links

The following poems in the *Climb Inside a Poem* big book are from observation:

"Singing Down the Sun" by Marilyn Singer p. 32

"Hidden Treasure" by Bobbi Katz p. 34

"Where Do I Find Poetry?" by Georgia Heard p. 2

"Spring Riddles" by Beverly McLoughland p. 29

Other texts that show writing from close observation of the world:

Byrd Baylor
The Other Way To Listen
Atheneum (1978)

Ralph Fletcher
Twilight Comes Twice
Clarion Books (1997)

Ralph Fletcher
Hello, Harvest Moon
Clarion Books (2003)

Kevin Henkes
All Alone
Greenwillow Books (2003)

Matthew Gollub
Cool Melons—Turn to Frogs!: The Life and Poems of Issa
Lee & Low Books (1998)

Aileen Fisher
Know What I Saw
Roaring Brook Press (2005)

Kristine O'Connell George
Hummingbird Nest: A Journal of Poems
Harcourt (2004)

David L. Harrison
Wild Country: Outdoor Poems for Young People
Boyds Mills Press (1999)

Joyce Sidman
Song of the Water Boatman & Other Pond Poems
Houghton Mifflin (2005)

Valerie Worth
Peacock and Other Poems
Farrar, Straus and Giroux (2002)

Rebecca Kai Dotlich
Lemonade Sun: And Other Summer Poems
Boyds Mills Press (1998)

Finding Inspiration in Poetry Itself

Read poems . . . then start writing down your own words.
Keep doing it. Keep doing it. Keep doing it.

—Joseph Bruchac

You can create a special place in the room where children can go to read (and write) poems during free moments throughout the day. To do this, you'll need to display poems at eye level on the wall for children to read, set up a basket of several familiar laminated poems, and make stacks or baskets of easily accessible poetry books. Include a journal or chart paper so students can write down the poetry books, poems, or words they have discovered and love.

You might instead create a poetry listening center. After all, listening to poetry is like laying a welcome mat in front of the door of poetry! You'll need, of course, a tape player or CD player and a few sets of headphones. You will need to make a tape recording of your favorite poems or buy recordings of poets reading their poems. Students can also record favorites. After listening, students might choose a favorite image to illustrate.

Minilesson

I've set up a special poetry place in the corner of the room so you can go there and read poems. There are individual poems you know well in a basket for you to read, and there are also poetry books in the basket. I'll keep searching for new poetry books, and every week I'll place them in the basket for you to read. If you find a poem you really love, copy it in your notebook, so you can keep it forever, and write the title in our class journal to recommend to other poetry readers in the class!

I've also put poetry paper and marking pens in the poetry place. If you're inspired to write your own poem after spending time reading poems, you'll have everything you need!

Book Links

These books can help you extend the minilesson.

Elise Paschen and others
Poetry Speaks to Children (book & CD)
Sourcebooks
MediaFusion; Har/Com edition (2005)

Jack Prelutsky
The Jack Prelutsky Holiday CD Audio Collection
HarperChildren's Audio (2005)

Shel Silverstein
Runny Babbit: A Billy Sook (book and abridged CD)
HarperCollins; Har/Com edition (2006)

Paul Fleischman
Joyful Noise/I Am Phoenix (audio cassette)
Audio Bookshelf (2001)

Bruce Degan
Jamberry (audio cassette)
HarperCollins (1996)

Mary Engelbreit
Mary Engelbreit's Mother Goose Book and CD
HarperCollins; Har/Com edition (2008)

Sharon Creech
Love That Dog (audiobook)
HarperChildren's Audio (2002)

[HarperChildren's Audio offers an array of children's books in CD and audio cassette formats.]

Finding Inspiration in Our Hearts

Many of my poems are about things I love so much that I feel I have to write about them. —Kristine O'Connell George

From the very beginning of the year, we ask young writers to write about what is important and meaningful to them. Sometimes it's difficult for them to access what is in their hearts. As a way of exploring what is meaningful, you can ask them to create "heartmaps." I created the idea of heartmapping when I realized that this activity can help young writers know and write what is important to them (see *Awakening the Heart* by Georgia Heard). A heartmap might include some of the following:

- Memories that we keep and that have stayed with us a long time
- People we love or who are meaningful to us
- Pets and what's special about our particular pet
- Hobbies or things we love to do
- Favorite things to do at home
- Special toys, perhaps stuffed animals that we've kept for a long time
- Special places where we feel loved and safe

For pre-k, kindergarten, and first grade, children can draw pictures first of what's in their hearts and then write letters or words to label their pictures. For older grades, I suggest children begin with writing words and then later draw pictures.

Children's heartmaps can be displayed on the bulletin board, taped on students' desks, or attached inside each writer's notebook. Although exploring what's in our hearts is often thought of as poetry's domain, all writing genres can be sparked by asking ourselves the question: "What really matters?"

Knowing what's in our hearts is the work of all writers. The purpose of creating heartmaps is to begin to come to know all those feelings and memories that will be the source of meaningful stories and poems later on in the year.

As you read poems to your students throughout the year, ask children to be on the lookout for poems they could attach to their heartmaps. Suggest that they listen for poems that relate to their lives or speak to them in a special way. For example, they might find a poem about something they love to do or about an experience they remember.

Minilesson

One of the things that a writer has to do before writing is to ask: "What do I really care about? What really matters to me that I could write my story or poem about?" Sometimes we forget what's important unless it's right there in front of us. Today we're going to be making heartmaps about the people and experiences that we really care about so that we can see and share those things that are meaningful to us. Let me show you an example. I've drawn a heart right here on this chart paper, and I'm going to draw and write inside my heartmap about what really matters to me. I have to ask myself first, "What is important to me that stays in my heart?" Hmmm. In the center, I'm going to write down "my family." Actually, I'm going to be detailed and name the people in my family.

Watch for a few minutes as I create my own heartmap on the chart paper. Now each one of you will make a heartmap for you to draw or write what's really important to you. Before you begin, let's sit for a moment and think about all those important experiences and people that you'll draw and write on your heartmap.

Book Links

These books can help you extend the minilesson.

Charlotte S. Huck
Secret Places
Greenwillow (1993)

Carol G. Hittleman
A Grand Celebration: Grandparents in Poetry
Boyds Mills Press (2002)

Cynthia Rylant
Waiting to Waltz: A Childhood
Atheneum/Richard Jackson Books (1984)

Lee Bennett Hopkins
Home to Me: Poems Across America
Orchard Books (2002)

Donald Graves
Baseball, Snakes, and Summer Squash: Poems About Growing Up
Boyds Mills Press (1996)

Finding Inspiration Around the Classroom

Think of the walls of your classroom as a HUGE poetry anthology! Instead of poems resting silently in a book, create "a living anthology of poems" (see *Awakening the Heart* by Georgia Heard) on the walls of your classroom. Displaying poems around the room teaches children that poetry can be woven throughout the everyday life of the classroom and that poems can be written about the ordinary things they use in school. Choose and display poems about common objects and school supplies—things that children know well. At the end of this minilesson, I've included several poems to display around the room to get you started.

Minilesson

Yesterday afternoon after you left school, I was very busy. I turned our classroom into a gigantic poetry anthology! A poetry anthology is a book filled with all kinds of poems. Hmm. Maybe you're asking, "How could our classroom become a book, especially a poetry anthology?" Well, I've sprinkled poems around the room—on walls, on school supplies, on shelves, and near the cubbies. You are going to find poems written about some of the things we use every day in class—the things that most people wouldn't even think that you could write a poem about. Let's go on a tour, and I'll read you some of these poems.

The first poem I want to read is about a pencil sharpener.

The Pencil Sharpener
By Georgia Heard

The pencil sharpener
chews
the pencil
into a sharp point
and spits
the leftovers out.

And over here, next to the paper clips, is a poem called "Paper Clips."

Paper Clips

By Rebecca Kai Dotlich

With tiny teeth
of tin
they take
one slender breath
before they make
a move,
and then—
a silver pinch!

With jaws
no bigger
than an inch
these dragon grips
are small and slight—
but
conquer pages
with
one
bite!

What do you think? Did you know that poems could be written about everyday things? Did you realize that poets look for the beauty and the poetry in even the most ordinary things?

I've provided some poetry paper here for you so that when you get inspired by something in the classroom, maybe you, too, can write a poem about it. Pretty soon, your poems will be sprinkled throughout the room with these others.

Let's make a list of some of the things in our classroom that you might want to write a poem about:

Poem Ideas in Our Room

- Pencil Sharpener
- Clock
- Pets (hermit crab, fish, gerbil, etc.)
- Computer
- Door

- Window
- Supplies (paper, pencils, erasers, crayons, scissors, etc.)
- Books
- Flag

Book Links

These books can help you extend the minilesson.

David L. Harrison
The Mouse Was Out at Recess
Boyds Mills Press (2003)

Carol Diggory Shields
Lunch Money: And Other Poems About School
Dutton Children's Books (1995)

Kay Winters
Did You See What I Saw?: Poems About School
Viking Juvenile (1996)

Lee Bennett Hopkins, editor
Good Books, Good Times!
Harper & Row (1990)

Lee Bennett Hopkins
School Supplies: A Book of Poems
Simon & Schuster (1996)

Reading Poetry

Introduction to Reading Poetry

The first-grade children have just walked in the classroom from the school bus. They are hanging their coats, hats, and mittens on hooks. They're taking off rain boots and putting on their shoes. They're shaking the rain from their hair.

Mrs. Mays walks to her rocking chair in the corner and waits for the children to settle in. When everyone is gathered on the rug for morning meeting, she whispers, "I found a poem that I thought would be perfect for today. Let me read it to you." The children are quietly waiting for the poem to begin. She begins to read "School Bus Lady" by J. Patrick Lewis (*Climb Inside a Poem* big book, p. 15).

She reads the poem once, slowly, and then reads it again, pausing in order to leave a circle of quiet around the poem. The children begin to talk among themselves, telling their stories of being on the school bus: the time they were late, the way the bus is always there at the same time every morning.

Every day at morning meeting, Mrs. Mays reads a new poem. Later on in the year, she'll read the same poem for several days—and even the same poem every day for a whole week—so the children can get to know that poem very well. Poems are displayed on the walls of the classroom, near the window, on the door, and next to the calendar. Several poems have become part of the classroom community. For example, to celebrate a child's birthday, the children always recite "Birthday Candles" by Rebecca Kai Dotlich (*Climb Inside a Poem* big book, p. 18). When a child loses a tooth, they chant in unison Lee Bennett Hopkins' "Tooth Truth" (big book, p. 7). Any time throughout the day, Mrs. Mays might call a "poetry break," and read aloud a poem she's found that she thinks they'll love. At the end of the day, when all the children are gathered together on the rug, Mrs. Mays might read "Night Story" by Beverly McLoughland (big book, p. 35).

In this community, poetry is not so rarified that it's only brought out in the spring. Poems are not just to teach children phonics, although there's no doubt that poetry can be very useful in teaching early oral and written language skills. Poetry is an integral part of the everyday life of the students. It's the chime that punctuates the transitions and events of the day. It's a light that illuminates the life of every child in the classroom. It's the bridge between two children sitting on opposite sides of the rug, who can't have a puppy. It's the door that invites the shyest girl in the class to speak what's on her mind and heart.

The poems the children hear every day will become part of what they know by heart. Knowing these poems, and being able to recite them, will help them build reading and writing fluency. The poems that they see and hear every morning will help them gain an intrinsic understanding of the ways print works; it will help build their natural instinct for syntax; it will help them build on their phonological and phonemic awareness.

In many primary classrooms, poetry is the daily bread—it's woven into the fabric of the everyday life of the classroom. The children begin to think in poetry, to speak and recite poetry, and to read and write poetry. The minilessons in this part of the book are meant to help you build a community like this. Section One presents minilessons to help you read aloud poetry across the whole school day. Section Two offers some suggestions for teaching structures that can help you support your youngsters in reading poetry aloud. It also offers some minilessons to help you support your children in starting to read poetry on their own.

SECTION 1
Reading Poetry Aloud to Children

If you are like me, you may not remember reading poems as a child, but you may remember hearing them. My mother would recite, "Pease porridge hot / Pease porridge cold / Pease porridge in the pot / Nine days old." She also sang us poem-songs, such as "Have you seen the muffin man, the muffin man, the muffin man . . .?" Nursery rhymes and other chants were like friends to us. We'd walk around the house singing them over and over again, carrying them wherever we went.

When I read poetry aloud to children, they sway back and forth, nod their heads, and clap their hands. They know the music of poetry because they feel it in their bodies. When I read non-rhyming poetry to children, it opens a window into a world outside of the classroom; it leads children to see the magic of the everyday, ordinary world all around them. We need to revive children's innate, natural responses to poetry. Does the poem make you want to get up and dance? Does it make you want to clap your hands to the beat? Does it give you pictures in your mind that will stay with you long after the poem is finished? Does it make you laugh out loud or shed a tear? Does it remind you of something that's happened to you in your own life?

In an effort to invite all children into the world of poetry, read to them. Read a poem to them every day. Reading poetry aloud gives children a model of fluent reading, and it provides a scaffold for language and literacy development. Perhaps the most important benefit in reading poetry aloud to children is in their oral language development. Listening to a poem a day helps children become readers and writers. A daily program of reading poetry aloud can help children with:

- Fluency
- Understanding how print works
- Phonological and phonemic awareness
- Comprehension
- Syntax

Following are a few simple rules to follow to help you make the most of reading poetry aloud to your children.

Essentials of Reading Poetry Aloud

1. **Select poems you think the children will love; select a variety of kinds of poems.**

   My experience with children is that they respond positively to a variety of poems: rhythmic and rhyming, repetitive and patterned, free verse, funny poems, serious poems, poems that tell a story, poems that use visual imagery and metaphor, and so on. Reading aloud a variety of poems helps children know that poetry, like music, has a variety of personalities, styles, and voices. In years past, children's experience with poetry was often limited to short, simple, repetitive, heavily rhymed chants and verses and to funny poems that would make them laugh. Children can understand far more than these! Imagine if we limited picture-book read alouds to short, rhyming texts! Open the world of poetry to young children, and you'll be surprised at the variety of poems to which they respond.

2. **Read each poem silently to yourself before reading it for the first time.**

   Once, I made the mistake of reading a poem aloud to a group of children when I'd never read the poem before. I thought the poem would be bright and bubbly—most of the poems by this poet are—so I read in a bright, singsong voice. As it turned out, the poem was about losing a cherished toy. My reading did not reflect the meaning or feeling of the poem, and the children were completely confused. I always recommend reading a poem silently first to decide how to read it aloud.

3. **Read each poem aloud more than once.**

   Because many poems are short and use more condensed language than a story, the initial experience of hearing a poem can happen in just a few seconds. In the first reading, children listen to the poem and may understand it, but hearing it a second time can help them absorb another layer of the poem. The second reading may give them time to understand more than they could at first. Explain to children that poems are meant to be read more than once and that each time they read or hear the poem again, they will understand more about it.

4. **Read each poem all the way through without interruption.**

   Before you begin reading the poem, talk with children about any difficult words that might block their understanding. The first time, read the poem all the way through without any interruptions so that children can absorb the whole poem at once. On third or fourth readings, you might choose to highlight a particular stanza, word, or part of the poem by reading only that part.

5. **When reading a poem, pay attention to its unique signals about how it should be read.**

   The way a poem looks on the page signals the way the poet wants the poem read. Include the title and author in your reading. Pause for a few seconds between the title and the poem's first line. When you read the poem aloud, pause briefly after line breaks, between stanzas, and at other places where the poet seems to call for space or silence—but make sure the rhythm doesn't sound choppy without cause. Decide where you need voice changes: where might you speak louder, more softly, in a whisper or a yell? Try it a few different ways to find the sound that is just right for each poem. Trust your ear.

6. **When reading a poem aloud, try to convey its personality, tone, and mood.**

   Every poem has a personality: some are quiet; some are loud; some are funny; some are contemplative; some are combinations. When you read a poem aloud, try to match the tone or the personality of the poem with your voice. For example, I wouldn't read most of Shel Silverstein's poems in a quiet monotone. Instead, I would let my tone and volume rise and fall with the build up and delivery of the joke or scenario. The mood of his poems, and of every poem, dictates how they should be read.

7. **Allow a circle of quiet to surround the reading of a poem.**

   The best ending to an initial reading of a poem is a few seconds of quiet. Let there be silence for a few beats after you finish reading; allow quiet to surround the poem. This will allow children to remain in the world of the poem and linger with the words and images and feelings for a moment.

Poetry in Daily School Life

Most of us receive a poem as a gift at least once a year. It's usually written by someone who works for a greeting card company, but it's a poem, nonetheless. People have always read poetry to celebrate special times or to express our feelings. We read poems for birthdays, anniversaries, holidays, and other occasions. We read poems to thank and to fume and to praise.

There are many ways to weave poetry into the cloth of daily school life. Below is a sample schedule. The left column lists parts of a school day typical for many elementary classrooms, and the right column suggests kinds of poems to be read at each time. Of course, everyone will have a different schedule, and you will need to adapt the poems to fit your day. Remember, it only takes a few minutes to read a poem. Who doesn't have time for that? Select the places and times where it makes sense for you to punctuate your day with a poem. I can guarantee that your students will fall in love with poetry.

Poetry Across the School Day Sample Schedule

Part of Day	*Kind of poem to read at that time*
Pledge of Allegiance	pledge poems: I wish . . . I hope . . .
Attendance	poems about starts or inspiring poems
Morning Circle	poems about friendship, special occasions, birthdays, losing a tooth
Reading Workshop	poems about reading and books
Writing Workshop	poems about writing and words
After recess	clear-the-mind, calming image poems
Lunch	food poems
Math	poems about numbers and calculating
Science/Social Studies	poems about the topic
Afternoon Circle	poems for nighttime and home and reflection on the day

You might plan to use these minilessons once or twice per week over the course of the fall and winter sessions. The minilessons are arranged here roughly from the most simple to the most complex, but this sequence is highly flexible, and we encourage you to choose the lessons that are right for your children at a given time.

Beginning the Day

Try to remember the poems you read or hear. The ones you love, that is, the few that really talk to you. You can forget about the rest. But those favorite poems you discover, fix them in your head. Try saying them back again, out loud or to yourself. Make them part of you. You'll find it becomes easier to write poems yourself, maybe poems that, if you're lucky, might become favorites of other people. —X. J. Kennedy

One important transition that happens every school day occurs in the morning when children leave the world of home and enter the world of school. We need to honor this important transition. Opening the day with a poem is a good way to set a reflective tone for the entire day. We can read poems about waking up, beginnings, mornings, or about anything that we know children will love.

Minilesson

Good morning, boys and girls! I'm going to be starting something new today that I'll be doing every day. I'm going to begin each day by reading a poem to celebrate the beginning of our wonderful day.

I'll read poems about waking up or things we do in the morning before school to get ready or about other things. But I'll need your help! If any of you read or hear a poem that you'd like to share to celebrate the beginning of the day, please let me know, and we can include that in our reading.

To begin, I'll read you one of my very favorite picture books, *The Way to Start a Day* by Byrd Baylor. It's a good way to remind us how people all over the world celebrate the beginning of the day.

Next, I'll read you a few examples of opening lines from the wonderful poems in *Wake Up, Sleepy Head!* by Mandy Ross.

Spider
Good morning, my babies.
This morning, it's time for your
Very first spinning lesson.

Dog
Sniff the morning
And sniff the dawn.
Scratch all over. . . .

Cow and Calf
Moooo!
Good morning to yoooou!

Book Links

These books can help you extend the minilesson.

Jack Prelutsky
For Laughing Out Loud: Poems to Tickle Your Funnybone
Knopf (1991). See "Learning" by Judith Viorst.

Georgia Heard, editor
This Place I Know: Poems of Comfort
Candlewick (2002). See "Commitment in a City" by Margaret Tsuda, "Dreams" by Langston Hughes, "Hold Fast Your Dreams" by Louise Driscoll, and "To You" by Karla Kuskin.

Carol Diggory Shields
Lunch Money: And Other Poems About School
Dutton Juvenile (1995). See "Eight-Oh-Three."

David L. Harrison
The Mouse Was Out at Recess
Boyds Mills Press (2003). See "The Bus."

Nikki Grimes
Thanks a Million
Amistad (2006). See "The Lunchroom," "Mystery," and "A Lesson from the Deaf."

Lillian Morrison
Whistling the Morning In: New Poems
Boyds Mills Press (1992)

Sharon Taberski, editor
Morning, Noon, and Night: Poems to Fill Your Day
Mondo Publishing (1996)

Mandy Ross
Wake Up, Sleepy Head!: Early Morning Poems
Child's Play International (2005)

Byrd Baylor
The Way to Start a Day
Atheneum (1978)

2 Pledging for the World

Many schools begin the day with the Pledge of Allegiance to the flag. Invite your children to join you in writing their own shared "pledge poem" that they can read after the Pledge of Allegiance, or find a poem or picture book to read aloud that can be recited as a class pledge. A pledge poem can be about ways that children can make the world a better, safer, more just place.

My son's elementary school participated in a nationwide Langston Hughes "dream" project, during which every student wrote their wishes for a better world and hung them around the classroom and school. Here is an example written by my son, Leo, when he was in Debi Gillert's wonderful first grade:

My Dream

By Leo O'Brien

Stop the oil pollution.
Oh please, Mother Nature sweep the world with love.
Help the world please.
I hope everyone is fantastically happy.
I hope creativity rules the world.
I hope for head to toes happiness
for all our fantastic citizens.
And that every citizen has justice
in your heart.
God is praying and watching over us.

Minilesson

Every morning we say the Pledge of Allegiance together. Does anyone know what a "pledge" is? It's a promise. I thought we could write our own shared pledge poem about how we could try to make the world a better place. We can even say our pledge poem together after we say the Pledge of Allegiance to the flag each day. Let me read you a pledge poem that children your age wrote:

Pledge

By Karen McKee's class

I wish the world was clean.
I will try to make it that way.
I wish there were no more wars,
that people would be nicer to each other.
I wish there were no more guns. No more violence.

I'm glad we have homes.
I will try and help those who don't.
I'm glad we have the world.

The poets in that class say their pledge poem every day after they say the flag pledge. I'm wondering what some of your thoughts and ideas are of what you could promise to try and do to help make our world a better place. I have chart paper ready here, and I thought we could write down some of our ideas of how we might make the world a better place to live, and then make a pledge poem that we could say every day. You might want to begin the lines of the poem with: I promise . . . I wish . . . I hope. . . .

I'm going to hang our pledge poem right here next to the flag. We can recite it together each morning after we say the Pledge of Allegiance.

Book Links

This book can help you extend the minilesson.

Georgia Heard, editor
This Place I Know: Poems of Comfort
Candlewick (2002). See "Ring Around the World" by Annette Wynne.

3 Easing Transitions

Try reading the same poem each time your children return from physical education, or each time they need to clean up or to leave the room together. You can read a poem to signal the time to line up for lunch, to go to the library, to prepare for art or music, and to get their brains ready for math or science or social studies. Let each poem become a signal to move into that area or that work.

Select the few poems that you will read in these times throughout the year. Post them on charts or half-sheets of poster board to be displayed while you read them. You might find it helpful to read these with a rhythm that could incorporate snapping or hand gestures. That type of activity will also help children go through the transition smoothly.

Minilesson

Instead of saying to you, "Okay, it's time for math!" or "It's time to line up for music," I'm going to read a certain poem to signal those times. In the morning, for example, when it's time to gather on the rug for reading, I'm going to signal that time by reading a particular poem—you'll hear it for the first time today. At different times during the day, as you're getting your things ready or gathering what you need for the next class, we will signal those times, too, with poems. I hope you'll learn the poems so we'll be able to say them together at each of these times!

Book Links

These books can help you extend the minilesson.

Lee Bennett Hopkins
Days to Celebrate: A Full Year of Poetry, People, Holidays, History, Fascinating Facts, and More
Greenwillow (2005). See "Two Lives are Yours" by Richard Armour.

Ralph Fletcher
A Writing Kind of Day: Poems for Young Poets
Boyds Mills Press (2005). See "Earth Head."

Arnold Adoff
Touch the Poem
Blue Sky Press (2000). See "When We Do Our Art."

Jack Prelutsky
For Laughing Out Loud: Poems to Tickle Your Funnybone
Knopf (1991). See "I Thought I'd Take a Rat to School" by Colin McNaughton.

David L. Harrison
The Mouse Was Out at Recess
Boyds Mills Press (2003). See "In The Hall" and "The Mouse Was Out at Recess."

Jack Prelutsky
The Random House Book of Poetry for Children
Random House (1983). See "Loose and Limber" and "No Girls Allowed."

Carol Diggory Shields
Lunch Money: And Other Poems About School
Dutton Juvenile (1995). See "Code," "Recess Rules," and "Spinning Song."

Carol Diggory Shields
Almost Late to School: And More School Poems
Dutton Juvenile (2003). See "B-Ball."

4 Setting Out for Lunch

Every morning as I was making and packing my son's lunch, I tried to write a poem to place in his lunchbox. Sometimes the poems were so bad that even my son commented on the quality (or lack of) of the poem that day. But sometimes, if my coffee was strong enough and I was lucky, I was able to write a decent "lunch poem."

Lunchtime poems aren't necessarily just for the lunchbox. They are meant to punctuate the time before, during, or after lunch. They can be about food, of course, but also about other lunchtime topics such as sitting and talking with friends, recess after the lunch period, and so on.

In a few of the schools I've visited, children and teachers have placed lunch poems on the backs of cafeteria chairs or on posters on the cafeteria walls to share with the entire school.

Minilesson

Some of my favorite poems to collect are about food. I'm going to share some of these poems with you now and every day before we go to lunch. We might even want to display some of our favorite food poems around the school. One class I know of posted food poems on the backs of the cafeteria chairs for students to read as they sat down for lunch.

Here is a poem about a gourmet lunch. It's called "Three Course Lunch."

Three Course Lunch
By Georgia Heard

1st course:
sandwich; raisins; chips.

2nd course:
water fountain sips.

3rd course:
jumps; swings; and skips.

Book Links

These books can help you extend the minilesson.

Jack Prelutsky
The Random House Book of Poetry for Children
Random House (1983). See "Table Manners" by Gelett Burgess.

Jack Prelutsky
For Laughing Out Loud: Poems to Tickle Your Funnybone
Knopf (1991). See "Never Take a Pig to Lunch" by Susan Alton Schmeltz.

Ralph Fletcher
A Writing Kind of Day: Poems for Young Poets
Boyds Mills Press (2005). See "Hungry for Poetry."

Carol Diggory Shields
Lunch Money: And Other Poems About School
Dutton Juvenile (1995). See "Swap," "Lunch Money," and "Decisions."

David L. Harrison
The Mouse Was Out at Recess
Boyds Mills Press (2003). See "Mystery Lunch."

Celebrating Occasions

You'll find some poems that you especially like. You might like to copy them into a notebook to make your own personal anthology. You'll find yourself reading and rereading these favorite poems and committing them to memory without even trying. These poems will be the best teachers you will ever have. They will show you how poems are made. —Beverly McLoughland

Children can celebrate their birthdays in school with a special poem to the birthday child. Teachers can collect birthday poems from which children can choose a favorite to read or for the class to recite, and the chosen poem may be sent home for families to read after school.

When a child loses a tooth in school, it's a big deal and a very special occasion—especially when it's a front tooth! We can celebrate and acknowledge this important occasion by reading a poem about losing a tooth. Teachers can include a copy of the tooth poem to send home with the child's tooth if he or she loses it during school. The class will come to know the poem by heart and recite their favorite tooth poem on their own. We've included two of our favorite tooth poems in the *Climb Inside a Poem* big book: "Tooth Truth" by Lee Bennett Hopkins (p. 7) and "Happy Teeth" by J. Patrick Lewis (p. 23). More wonderful birthday poems can be found in the Book Links.

Minilesson

Boys and girls, today is a special day. It's ____'s [name] birthday. I'm going to read you a very special poem to celebrate. I've made copies of the poem to send home for you to read at home. I've started a collection of birthday poems so each time it's someone's birthday, we have a selection of poems from which to choose.

Book Links

These books can help you extend the minilesson.

Jack Prelutsky
Read a Rhyme, Write a Rhyme
Knopf (2005). See "If We Didn't Have Birthdays" by Dr. Seuss, "Birthday" by Myra Cohn Livingston, and "Birthdays" by Mary Ann Hobermann.

Lee Bennett Hopkins
Days to Celebrate: A Full Year of Poetry, People, Holidays, History, Fascinating Facts, and More
Greenwillow (2004). See "The Year" by Felice Holman.

Lee Bennett Hopkins
Happy Birthday
Simon and Schuster (2000)

Welcoming People

Sometimes a child needs a little help in making the transition from home to school after being sick for a day or more. On the first day back to class, students can recite a "welcome back" poem to the student returning to school. A welcome back poem can be about friendship, or about missing someone, or it can be simply a poem that the child loves. Or you could share "Welcome Back!", the very simple poem I wrote for Mrs. Hig's second-grade class and included in the lesson below.

In Mrs. Hig's class, when Griffin came back to school after missing a couple of weeks, the class recited "Welcome Back!" and added these lines for him: "We missed your brainyness. / Gizzy (the class pet lizard) missed you too."

Griffin beamed as the class read the poem.

Minilesson

We all know that the class just doesn't seem complete when one of you is sick and at home. For the person coming back to class after being sick, sometimes you might feel a little homesick coming back to school after being at home. So, I thought that whenever someone returns to school after being absent, we could say a poem together to welcome him or her back. Here's a poem by Georgia Heard that we can say together, and we can even add our own words to it:

Welcome Back!
By Georgia Heard
We missed you!
The class just didn't feel right
without you.

We missed your smile!
We missed your laughter!
We missed your (*something special about the person*).
We missed your (*something special about the person*).

Your seat was lonely
without you.
We missed you!
Welcome back!

Book Links

These books can help you extend the minilesson.

Carol Diggory Shields
Lunch Money: And Other Poems About School
Dutton Juvenile (1995). See "Code."

Jack Prelutsky
The Random House Book of Poetry for Children
Random House (1983). See "*Measles*" by Kaye Starbird.

Jack Prelutsky
For Laughing Out Loud: Poems to Tickle Your Funnybone
Knopf (1991). See "The Water's Deep" by Colin McNaughton.

Jack Prelutsky
Read a Rhyme, Write a Rhyme
Knopf (2005). See "My First Best Friend" by Jack Prelutsky, "I Remember, I Remember," by Dennis Lee, and "Wait for Me" by Sarah Wilson.

Kay Winters
Did You See What I Saw?: Poems About School
Viking Juvenile (1996). See "Lots of Spots," "Runny Nose," and "Blizzard."

Setting a Tone

Read the funny poems, the zany verses that make you laugh—but don't stop there. Read the lovely, the sad, the mysterious. . . . Read poems that rhyme and don't rhyme. Notice the rhythm of the words and the patterns of the lines. And never read a poem only once. —Alice Schertle

I've heard teachers proclaim poetry breaks randomly during the day. The class might need a poetry break when they've been concentrating for a long time and need to freshen their minds. After recess, when the children are full of playful energy and need to focus on schoolwork, is a perfect time for a poetry break. Poems can set all kinds of tones, of course, but teachers often choose to read calming poems—poems kids will have to lean into and listen to closely; poems about small, quiet things; poems with relaxing feelings in them.

Minilesson

I was thinking that poems can be little, relaxing breaks we can take using words. Throughout the day, I'm going to be reading a poem whenever I feel we need a little break. We can stretch, breathe deeply, and let the poem calm us and take us on a refreshing trip to a new place in our minds.

Book Links

The following poems in the *Climb Inside a Poem* big book have a strong tone:

"Hidden Treasure" by Bobbi Katz p. 34

"Night Story" by Beverly McLoughland p. 35

Other texts with strong tone:

Georgia Heard
Songs of Myself: An Anthology of Poems and Art
Mondo Publishing (2000)

Rebecca Kai Dotlich
When Riddles Come Rumbling: Poems to Ponder
Boyds Mills Press (2001)

Jack Prelutsky
If Not for the Cat
Greenwillow (2004)

Jack Prelutsky
Read a Rhyme, Write a Rhyme
Knopf (2005). See "Bursting."

Jack Prelutsky
The Random House Book of Poetry for Children
Random House (1983.) See "Thoughts on Talkers" by Walter R. Brooks.

X. J. Kennedy and Dorothy Kennedy
Talking Like the Rain: A Read-to-Me Book of Poems
Little, Brown (1992)

Closing the Day

Poetry is especially appropriate for our "hurry-up and go" culture because it is so short. Most children's poems take less than 30 seconds to read. And yet the whole range of emotions is there . . . jealousy, hurt feelings, meanness, joy, silliness, wonder. There are poems on every subject: cars, dinosaurs, trees, dreams, superstitions, sports, teddy bears. —Janet Wong

Ending the day with a poem helps ease the transition from school to home. You can select poems about night or nighttime, sleep or bedtime, or even homework to send children home from school.

Poetry can help children get to know each other, as well as encourage empathy and support among each other. Poems about friendship, feelings, treating others with kindness, or any other subject that children have in common can help build a community feeling in a classroom and inspire conversations.

Minilesson

One of the most wonderful qualities about poetry is that we can share poems together about what we're feeling. The most amazing thing is that poems can make us feel like all of us have a lot in common. Sometimes I'll read a poem and many of us will say, "I feel that way too!" And so, at the end of each day, I'm going to be sharing poems out loud about some of the things you might be feeling or experiencing throughout the day—feelings and things that might be difficult to talk about or hard to find words for. I'll be looking for poems about friendship and what it means to be a friend, poems about having a good day or a bad day . . . any poems that have to do with feelings and experiences that we all have in common.

I'd like to have a conversation around these poems, to help us name some of our own feelings and to know that even someone in the class that you've never really talked to may feel the same way inside as you do!

I'm going to start by reading a poem about friendship called "Best Friend" by Marilyn Singer (*Climb Inside a Poem* big book p. 17).

Book Links

These texts can help you extend the minilesson.

"Hurt No Living Thing"
by Christina Rosetti (1872).
Available online. Also in *The Complete Poems* by Christine Rosetti, R.W. Crump, and Betty S. Flowers, Penquin Classics (2001).

Mary Ann Hoberman
You Read to Me, I'll Read to You: Very Short Stories to Read Together
Little, Brown Young Readers (2001). See "I Like."

Jack Prelutsky
Read a Rhyme, Write a Rhyme
Knopf (2005). See "Wait for Me," "I Remember," "My First Best Friend," and "Lonely."

Lee Bennett Hopkins
Days to Celebrate: A Full Year of Poetry, People, Holidays, History, Fascinating Facts, and More
Greenwillow (2005). See "Treasured Words."

Georgia Heard
This Place I Know: Poems of Comfort
Candlewick (2002). See "Ring Around the World," "This Place," and "Stars."

Carol Diggory Shields
Almost Late to School: And More School Poems
Dutton Juvenile (2003). See "Friend."

Eloise Greenfield
In the Land of Words: New and Selected Poems
Amistad (2003). See "Making Friends."

Eloise Greenfield
The Friendly Four
Amistad (2006)

Nikki Grimes
Thanks a Million
Amistad (2006)

SECTION 2
Supporting Children in Reading Poetry Aloud

When I work with children reading poetry—whether they are working independently, in pairs, in small groups, or in clubs, I naturally want to focus them on the sound of poetry. I want to coach them into noticing and learning from each poem's spacing, tone, intensity, and mood. Yet, I realize that no matter what text we are reading, we must focus on making meaning or there is no reading going on. It is helpful to remember that comprehension is more than just giving the "right" answers to someone else's questions. Comprehension is making connections, building personally relevant understandings, wondering and noticing, and learning to question the text and the writer.

Through the minilessons in this guide and through the *Climb Inside a Poem* lessons working with a poem across the week, you will be leading your readers toward this identity. They will come to approach poems with a sense of wonder and a keen eye and ear for noticing. They will come to poems with the clear expectations of making sense, building connections, and naturally questioning the writer's intentions. So, when you begin presenting poems for paired reading and small group work in poetry clubs, remind your young readers that you will be listening in as they engage in conversations about the poems they are reading. Let them know you'll be listening for their connections. That means you will expect to hear phrases such as:

- This poem reminds me of the time when I . . .
- This poem reminds me of the time when my family . . .
- This poem reminds me of the time when my friends . . .
- This poem is like the poem called ___________ because . . .
- This poem is like the book called ___________ because . . .
- This poem is like the story called ___________ because . . .
- This poem makes me think of something I know about . . .
- This poem makes me think of something I heard on the news . . .

Also, you will be listening for their observations, so you'll be expecting to hear phrases such as:

- I noticed this poem uses rhyming words . . .
- I noticed the poet paints word pictures when she says . . .
- I noticed that when you read this poem aloud, you can hear the beat. Listen, it goes like this . . .

- I noticed the poet uses a simile when she compares . . . (e.g., the warmth of the sun to being near a friend)
- I noticed the poet uses a metaphor when he says . . . (e.g., the moon is a glowing pearl)

While poems from the *Climb Inside the Poem* big book will provide inviting, familiar text to the emergent readers, and a bit of support for developing readers, your more proficient readers may enjoy the challenge of new poetry in their reading diet. The Book Links I have layered in throughout the guidebook and the lessons will be a good way to provide more challenging material for those who are ready to move forward. And, of course, you can pair a more proficient reader with a developing reader to share a poem as one reads to the other.

Reading poetry independently, in pairs, and in small groups can strengthen "reading muscles" over time. Through poetry children have many opportunities for making inferences, noticing, wondering, making connections, extending vocabulary, and building their repertoire of strategies for making sense of unfamiliar words. Poetry, because it is presented in small "doses," reduces the tension that some readers associate with longer and denser texts. In short, poetry can be less intimidating for many young readers.

So if your children are ready to begin reading poems independently, it is safe to assume that you and your students have been swaying to the rhythm of poetry, dancing and clapping and snapping to the beat, reading poetry together in one voice, and playfully alternating voices as you help them discover the rich language of poetry. By this time your young poets have written poems along with you, and some students have written poems independently. They have "climbed inside" poems as they interpreted the words through their art and rhythms and dance or movement. They have lived with poems now, and poetry has become part of the ritual and routine of the classroom community. By now, neither you nor your students could imagine a day without poetry.

Setting Up

Now let's invite your young poets to explore poems alone, with a partner, or together as a small group or in a longer-lasting poetry club. You will find that individual copies of poems from both the *Climb Inside a Poem* big book and selected Book Links will make wonderful texts for independent, paired, and small group reading.

One way to set up for independent, paired, and small group poetry-reading work is to make tape recordings of the poems to accompany individual copies of the poems you will provide. Emergent, developing, and struggling readers will continue to need the support of your voice to read the poem's words or at least to establish a pace and tone appropriate for each poem. Hearing your voice provides a sort of "training wheels" transition for reading the poem on their own next time; it is that bit of added support that will help them move toward reading the poems independently.

To set up support for individual readers, provide the recording with one set of headphones and a stack of copies of the recorded poems for note-taking. To provide the same support for a small group, write the selected poems on large-size chart paper and laminate it or cover it with clear contact paper. A small group of poetry readers can now gather around the chart and follow along as the recorder plays your voice out loud. One child in the group can use a pointer to track the print as your voice and the group read along. This set up is much like the choral readings your class has become accustomed to! That small bit of support may be all that is needed to move a few readers along the path toward independence.

Word Work

Let's take a look at what kind of work we might see as a small group gathers around a chart. After reading along with your recorded voice, the children use dry-erase pens to circle the rhyming words—each set with a new color. The children make observations and ask questions about the rhyming pairs. They might notice and ask why some rhyming words share a spelling pattern (gr*ound*/m*ound*, *sand*/h*and*) while other pairs have the same sound with different spellings (h*eart*/st*art*). This sort of exploration deepens children's insights and understandings about language. To record these understandings, group members can sign the chart and you can take a digital photo of their work before they spray the surface with a window cleaner and wipe away their writing to clear space for a new exploration.

Children might also decide to work with a poem by changing the rhyming pairs to make a different version of the poem. It might happen that you would need to remind them that the poem has to make sense! Poems are not just rhymes! Again, as they finish, you could record their thinking with a quick digital photo.

There are many different ways that children can engage in word work with poetry:

- They can look for, circle, and study instances of alliteration. What is the repeated sound? What are the ways to spell that sound? Why might the poet have chosen to use that technique here?
- Children might use the poems to identify and note instances of phonetic patterns they are studying at other times of the day. They might note instances of initial consonant blends, for example, or *-ing* endings.

- The rhythmic quality of many poems makes them perfect for children practicing syllabification. They might clap out the poems and try to mark where syllables fall.
- Children can circle and discuss new vocabulary words, words they love, words that create a strong feeling or image or tone, or words they want to collect for their own writing.

Early Reading Work

Emergent readers may not yet be able to point to the specific word of the poem they are listening to from the tape. Instead, they will use the pointer in a general way. This reading play is essential for growth; we need to support their reading approximations. Leave the *Climb Inside a Poem* big book open on an easel to invite spontaneous reading. A few of the poems in the big book are especially appropriate for emergent readers: "Happy Toes" and "Quack, Quack" by Pat Mora, "Making Soup" by Marilyn Singer, and "How I Hopscotch" by Kristine O'Connell George. These poems provide more scaffolding for the reading experience than some others. For example:

- The repetition in "Happy Toes" and "Quack, Quack" is predictable and therefore easier to read.
- The sequence of counting in "Quack, Quack" is predictable.
- The steps to preparing and playing hopscotch in "How I Hopscotch" are predictable to those who know the game.
- The chanting rhythm of "How I Hopscotch" and "Making Soup" makes it easier to guess what the next words will be.

Interpretive Work

Another kind of work children might take on with a poem is interpretation-based work. Children might take the laminated poem chart to a spot in the room where they can spread out around it. As they read it together with a recording of your voice, one child could use the pointer to track the print. They could use their dry-erase pens, not to circle rhymes this time, but instead to circle the lines of the poem that they think are the most important ones, or to write thoughts about the heart of the poem. Then they might talk together about their choices for most important words and their thoughts. Once again you could record their work with a digital photo of the chart before asking them to clean the chart for the next readers. Other questions children can ask themselves that help them interpret the poem could be:

- What happens in this poem? Why do I think so?
- What does this poem mean? Why do I think so?
- What is the one picture I could draw that would show what the whole poem is about? Why would that be the one picture instead of some other possibility?
- What is one word that is the heart of the poem? Why would I choose that word?
- What is the poet saying about life? How can I tell?
- Why did the poet write this poem? What was she/he trying to say? Why do I think so?

Collaborative Work

When children work collaboratively in poetry clubs, their work might look a bit different than that described above. While independent work, paired work, and small group work might only last one or two days, poetry clubs tend to be a longer-lasting commitment to one poem or set of poems by a small group of children. In a poetry club, children of similar interest gather together to read a poem or set of poems and host conversations about them. The group may select books together, or the group may form because someone selects a theme or topic or title and then invites others to "join the club!" Once the children have had time to read the poem and prepare for their conversation together—either by thinking a bit or by jotting notes to themselves—the club can meet and talk together. The conversation could focus on the readers' observations and questions and connections. In a poetry club, we expect poetry readers to talk openly, share insights, and sometimes politely challenge one another's thinking.

In a poetry club, you might think of each brain as a flower and each voiced idea as a bee. As the ideas buzz around the group, the flowers get pollinated and new thinking blossoms from that. So in each meeting, young children are encouraged to come with their connections and insights, their interpretations, and their confusions and wonderings. As members of a poetry club, readers are challenged to push their thinking, to grow new ideas and see new connections. Readers should leave each meeting of a poetry club more equipped to read alone, to make deeper and more robust meaning from each subsequent reading experience. From participation in a poetry club, children can learn:

- ". . . that comprehension is more than giving the 'right' answers to someone else's questions
- . . . that comprehension is more a process of making sense of what is read than a process of finding the answer on the page

- . . . that sharing differing perspectives broadens the views of everyone and deepens the insights of all who participate
- . . . to read with an open mind seeking broader points of view, questioning the ideas of the writer, seeking to make sense of what is read, and to go beyond the details on the page
- . . . to value their own ideas and to respect the views of others even if they are different from their own." (L. Laminack, 1998, *Volunteers Working With Young Readers*. Urbana, IL: NCTE, p. 20)

Fluency: Helping Children Get Started Reading Poetry on Their Own

Whether your children will work independently, in pairs, in small groups, or in poetry clubs, and whether they are experienced readers or just learning to read, they will need to learn a few basics about how to read poetry fluently. The following minilessons are designed to help children learn to get started reading poetry on their own.

Reading Line Breaks

A poem, like a gift, becomes the reader's own.

—Rebecca Kai Dotlich

A fluent reading calls for much more than speed. A fluent reading calls for more than getting all the words right. Reading a poem fluently is about recognizing and interpreting the music and the meaning in the language. It's about being able to read expressively and with understanding. Reading poetry is a perfect opportunity for you and your young readers to practice reading fluently through individual or choral readings.

Minilesson

Today I want to talk to you about how we read poetry a little differently from how we read a story. I just read Rebecca Kai Dotlich's poem "Birthday Candles" to you, and I want to stop and talk to you about the way I read it.

I'm going to read the poem aloud again as if it were written like a story without the lines and line breaks, and I want you to notice how it sounds.

> "Today I am the star of birthdays! Of ice cream, of cake, of candles. I get one secret wish, (here comes my favorite part . . .) whoossshhhhh, whew! Those candle flames go out, but the wish stays in my heart."

Without the lines and line breaks, there are no signals to tell me how the poem should be read.

Now I'm going to read the poem with the line breaks, which are signals for the reader to pause slightly after every line. Whenever you see white space in the poem, that signals you to pause and be silent for just a little bit. I'm going to read the poem out loud, paying attention to the signals. See if you notice a difference in the sound of it this time compared to the first time I read it like a story. As I read, I'll write the poem on this chart paper so you can see, and I'll write some signals in brackets at the end of each line.

Today	[*slight pause*]
I am the star	[*slight pause*]
of birthdays!	[*full stop*]
Of ice cream,	[*slight pause*]

of cake,	[*slight pause*]
of candles.	[*full stop*]
I get one secret wish,	[*slight pause*]
(here comes my favorite part . . .)	[*slight pause*]
whoossshhhhh, whew!	[*full stop*]
Those candle flames go out,	[*slight pause*]
but the wish stays in	[*slight pause*]
my heart.	[*full stop*]

Notice how Rebecca Kai Dotlich wrote the word *Today* on a line all by itself; when a word stands alone like that, it signals to the reader that this word is very important. Each line and line break in a poem has a reason behind it.

The difference you hear between the first time I read the poem and the second time is the music and feeling of poetry. Poetry depends on the signals of white space around the words.

Interpreting the Poem's Sound

I read all kinds of poems and memorized some of them, not because I was forced to, but because I loved the sound of the words so much. —Beverly McLoughland

Recognizing signals in the text and attending to tone, mood, pacing, the intensity of the language, and the intentions of the poet is what fluency is all about. That recognition can lead young readers toward greater confidence, toward greater control over written language, and toward more effective, more efficient, and more fluent reading.

Minilesson

Let's take a look at the poem "Birthday Candles" by Rebecca Kai Dotlich once again. This time, let's look at the feeling and mood of the poem. What feeling do you think the poet wanted to give us? Excitement, happiness, eagerness? We can imagine that the speaker in the poem feels bright and upbeat because it's her birthday. So I'm going to read it aloud one more time. Think about the signals in the poem as you listen, and we will talk about what you notice.

Today	[slight pause]	Note the exclamation mark that ends this thought.
I am the star	[slight pause]	This is a moment of joy
of birthdays!	[full stop]	and excitement. Your voice must
Of ice cream,	[slight pause]	reflect those emotions.
of cake,	[slight pause]	The feeling, then, suggests a
of candles.	[full stop]	level of excitement that
I get one secret wish,	[slight pause]	may be a bit louder than your normal speaking voice.
(here comes my	[slight pause]	You might want to read the
favorite part . . .)		words in parentheses in a
whoossshhhhh, whew!	[full stop]	quieter voice.
Those candle flames	[slight pause]	The poem winds down as the
go out, but the wish	[slight pause]	wish goes up and the flames
stays in my heart.	[full stop]	go out, so the voice will slow and become quieter.

Wow! Doesn't the poem sound stronger and make more sense when we read it as the poet wanted the poem to be read? I think we are getting close to how she heard the poem in her mind as she wrote it. Whenever you read a poem, be sure to pay attention to the signals that the poet gives as to how he or she wants the poem read.

Finding Reading Signals from the Page

When I taught this fluency lesson in Mrs. Hig's second-grade room, we came up with the idea of children playing the "poetry conductor" to guide us in reading the poem aloud—just as in an orchestra there is a conductor guiding the musicians in playing music. One morning, Luke, the poetry conductor for the day, stood beside the poem "Birthday Candles," and, using a pointer, pointed to the words in the poem as the students read them out loud; he was "conducting" the poem as if it were music. Whenever the poem signaled for their voices to come to a full-stop (either after a line with a period or between stanzas), Luke put up his hand with palm facing out to remind the students to stop reading and to pause for a moment. The children were so excited at this new poetry job that everyone in the class wanted to play the "poetry conductor."

You might also give each student a copy of a poem and have them write signals on it to show how they think the poem should be read. The class can make up their own symbols for signals, such as a picture of a stop sign for a full-stop, a yellow "yield" sign for a slight pause, a rising line for higher volume, and a falling line or *shhh!* for a lower voice.

In Mrs. Hig's class, Uma and Bella came up with the following signals to write on "Sky Wish":

- Red dot for stop at the end of the poem
- Yellow triangle for slow for most stanzas
- Red half-note for soft voice
- Green half-note for high voice
- And a yellow star for special attention

The girls' way of reading the poem showed they understood the tone of the poem: the hyphen after *string* was marked with a yellow triangle as a kind of "pause and slow down" signal, and the line ". . . my wish came true" was marked by green half-notes meaning that the reader needed to read this line with a high, excited tone. Their yellow star by the ellipsis after *fly* was a special signal—meaning that the reader needed to extend her voice for a little while before reading the next line.

Other children came up with up and down arrows for raising and lowering voices; red, yellow, and green kites for stop, slow down, and go; and a long kite tail that was meant to show how the reader needed to stretch her voice after "fly . . ." to the beginning of the next line. Ryan invented a new word, "slop," to indicate that the reader should stop and slow down at the same time, such as after a line break with a punctuation mark like a comma or a semicolon.

Minilesson

Poets, we've been talking together about how to read a poem's signals of how to read it out loud. Well, I was thinking about some of the signals that we see every day on street signs telling us when to stop and slow down. What are some of the signals that we see on the street? Yes, a red sign for *stop*, yellow for *slow*, and green for *go*.

I was thinking that a poem has signals, too, that tell us how to read it. Sometimes the signals are easy to read, like a line break means *pause*—but sometimes the poem wants us to slow down or lower our voice or read with a particular feeling, and the signals are less obvious.

Today, work with your reading partner and read "Sky Wish" together again. Together, invent your own signals for how to read the poem. You can use colored pencils, and you can use street-sign colors or make up your own signs.

Writing Poetry

Writing Poetry
Introduction: Essentials for Launching a Poetry Writing Unit

Don't be polite.
Bite in.
Pick it up with your fingers . . .
—from "How to Eat a Poem" by Eve Merriam

Now that children have clapped their hands and danced to the rhythm of poems, closed their eyes and stepped into magical worlds as they've listened to poems—they're ready for the next step: writing poetry and becoming poets themselves. Many of them have already become poets! Unlike in "Reading Poetry," the minilessons in this section are a cohesive unit and are meant to be used in the sequence in which they are presented, each lesson directly following the other with no other writing lessons interspersed.

Have fun, and be open to all the wonderful poetry that will blossom in your class in the next few weeks! I hope you keep in mind Eve Merriam's wonderful words above as you begin your "Writing Poetry" unit of study.

You'll be amazed at all the wonderful, insightful, inspiring poems that your students will write!

Essentials for Launching a Poetry Writing Unit

- **For pre-k and kindergarten students, wait until spring to introduce poetry writing.** Young writers need to get used to writing, and waiting also gives you time to immerse children in poetry-rich language from read alouds and discussions about poems. In the spring, when young writers feel comfortable with writing and they've listened to a variety of poems, they will be eager and feel more successful when they begin to write their own.
- **Spend 2 to 5 weeks on writing poetry**. A sample poetry writing daily schedule looks like this:
  - Minilesson 5–10 minutes
  - Independent writing time 20–30 minutes
  - After-the-workshop share time 5–10 minutes

- **Show and read poems written by children in children's handwriting to your class.** You'll find examples provided throughout this guidebook. Seeing the actual writing of other children their age reminds young poets to use invented spelling when they need to, to get their thoughts on the page. It also shows children that poems don't have to look like the ones in a published book. Showing children other children's wonderful poetry sends the message: "You can do it!"
- **Make "poetry paper" easily available to everyone.** Changing the shape of traditional paper to suggest long, lean, poetry-shaped writing encourages children to write in lines and stanzas rather than in sentences and paragraphs. To make poetry paper, you could cut lengthwise strips of lined or unlined pastel or white paper. Make sure you explain that sometimes poems look like tall buildings, and show examples of long lean poems from the *Climb Inside a Poem* big book. You might also use unlined, 11″ × 17″, legal-sized paper turned so that it, too, is tall and thin. This gives children room to draw pictures, experiment with word placement, and change a poem's shape.
- **Ask very young poets to write a "P" at the top of the page, declaring their intention to write a poem rather than a story.** This will help get them into the mindset of writing poems, and it will alert you to the genre in which they are trying to write.
- **Make poetry folders in which poets can store their poems and poetry-related pictures and writing.** Pocket folders are best, since long poetry paper can easily slip out of regular folders. You might ask children to:
  - illustrate their folder covers with heartmaps (see "Part One: Creating a Poetry-Rich Environment" p. 29)
  - tape a favorite poem on the cover
  - tape an illustration of their favorite poem on the cover
  - draw images or tape photos of their favorite people and things on the cover to inspire themselves
- **Refer to the children in your class as "poets."** Call them to the rug area for share time by saying, *"Poets, please gather on the rug for share time."* Or, in a minilesson, say, *"I've noticed that all the poets in this class have been working very hard on their poems. . . ."* Hearing themselves referred to as poets invites them into the world of poetry.
- **After the minilesson, occasionally ask a child to talk briefly to the class about what she or he is going to do as a poet that day.** These quick talks can model for other students the process of poetry writing, whether it's modeling finding a topic for a poem, modeling brainstorming a good simile, or modeling any other part of the process.
- **Let children know from the first day onward that when they're finished writing their poems, they have new work to do.** Since the poems that young poets

write are usually very short (especially in the beginning), it's essential for class management reasons that you take a few minutes to explain what your young poets can do when they finish writing each of their poems. You might say, *"Over the next few weeks, you're going to be writing bunches of poems. That's what poets do: they write poems and then pick the ones they want to share and celebrate. You have your special poetry folders to keep your poems in. We're going to be writing and learning poems for a few weeks, so you'll have many poems from which to choose for our poetry celebration!"*

Here are some of the things you can have students do when they finish writing a poem:

- Write the title and your name.
- Illustrate the poem.
- Read your poem to yourself and a partner.
- Place it in your poetry folder.
- Get a new piece of poetry paper and begin a new poem.

Sharing Children's Own Poetry

Poets will be excited and eager to share their poems right after they've written them. After writing time, leave 5 or 10 minutes for a Poet's Share. Set up a Poet's Chair for one poet to sit in as the other poets gather closely around on the rug. Kids can decorate the back and arms of the Poet's Chair by taping on favorite poems, illustrations of favorite poems, quotes about poetry, or special lines from poems. Decorating can extend to the area around the Poet's Chair, too.

Choose two or three poets to share to the class from the Poet's Chair. Then ask the poets sitting on the rug to each share with a partner. Having both kinds of shares is important so that all students can celebrate the poems they've written that day.

Tips for Poetry Sharing

- The purpose of after-workshop sharing of poems is to celebrate students' efforts—to point out what the poet has done well and to model for other students. There is no critique during sharing time, just questions to clarify the meaning or to find out more information.
- Poets who are reading a poem should read it twice because poems are short and over quickly. It helps the listeners to hear a poem a second time.

- Listening poets can close their eyes to help them listen and picture the words. Sometimes, several listening poets can share the images they saw in their minds as they listened.
- Listening poets can listen for any special, unusual, surprising words or ways of describing things, and share their finds.
- Listening poets can listen and tell the poet what the poem made them feel.
- Add new things learned about poetry from the share time to the What We Know About Poetry chart. (See Minilesson 1: "What Do We Know About Poetry?" p. 76.)

SECTION 1
Inspiration

Inspiration for poetry writing comes from so many places. It's important for children to realize that an idea for a poem can come from anywhere:

- from another poem or poet
- from observing the world around them, big and small
- from inside their hearts, or their own feelings

What Do We Know About Poetry?

Poems will be the best teachers you will ever have. They will show you how poems are made. —Beverly McLoughland

Set the stage for exploring poetry with children. The following minilesson is a good way to assess what children have absorbed from listening and discussing poems so far during the year; their ideas and comments can guide your teaching. For example, if your students say, "All poems rhyme," you'll know you should read them more non-rhyming poems! As students remember and learn more and more about poetry, add their observations to an ongoing list—a list you start in this minilesson. In one first-grade class, young poets said they knew this about poetry:

It rhymes but it doesn't have to.
Poems repeat words.
It's usually short.
Poems come from the heart.
Poems use special words.
Poems have a beat.

Minilesson

All year long, we've been reading poems together, sharing our favorites, and some of you have even started writing your own poems. Now, we're all going to be poets! For the next few weeks, we're going to be writing poems and learning more about poetry. At the end of a few weeks, we'll celebrate the poems you've written.

You've listened to, and we've read, many poems, so let's start with remembering what we know about poetry. Who wants to share some things you know about poetry for me to write on this chart?

Poets! This is so exciting! You know a lot about poetry so far, and we're going to be learning even more as you write your own poems.

Extensions

- The What We Know About Poetry chart can be posted near the sharing area, and you and your class can keep adding to it. At the end of each week, as a minilesson, you can spend a few minutes reviewing what new things they've learned about poetry that can be added to the chart.

- As you continue to read poems out loud, you can add the titles of particular poems alongside the qualities of poetry on the What We Know About Poetry chart. For example, you might write "How I Hopscotch," by Kristine O'Connell George, next to "Poems have a beat." "Singing Down the Sun," by Marilyn Singer, might go next to "Poems use special words."
- Near the end of the poetry writing unit, you might want to take a fresh page of chart paper and gather the most important things from the What We Know About Poetry chart to keep as a guideline in the classroom for next year.

Book Links

These books can help you extend the minilesson.

Eloise Greenfield
In the Land of Words: New and Selected Poems
HarperCollins (2004)

Lee Bennett Hopkins
Good Books, Good Times!
HarperTrophy (1990)

Paul Janeczko
The Place My Words Are Looking For: What Poets Say About and Through Their Work
Simon & Schuster (1990)

Paul Janeczko
Seeing the Blue Between: Advice and Inspiration for Young Poets
Candlewick (2002)

Advice from Our Favorite Poets

Looking for poem subjects is a bit like going fishing—you wait for the tug on the line and then you reel in your catch—not a fish, but a poem! —Patricia Hubbell

There are many different doors into the world of writing poetry—and every poet has to find her or his own way in. Reading about where other poets find ideas for writing a poem is inspiring, and can lead us to find our own ideas for a poem.

Minilesson

Poets, I'd like to read to you what other poets say about where they get ideas for writing poems. Listen carefully as I read these poets' words, and we can talk and see if you got any ideas from these poets.

Where Do Poets Get Their Ideas?

Marilyn Singer says, "Pay attention to the world around you—little things, big things, people, animals, buildings, events, etc. What do you see, hear, taste, smell, feel?"

Rebecca Kai Dotlich says, "Always, find wonder in your world. Look—really look at that frog near the pond, that bus rumbling down the road, that sunflower towering over the fence, that puddle shimmering in the field, that tiny paper clip on the desk. Open your eyes and your heart to all the senses, all the imaginings, all the words and images in the world."

Jane Yolen says, "Sometimes a line runs through my head 'Oh, world, I wish . . .' and a poem comes from that."

Patricia Hubbell says, "Pay attention to everything. Ask questions, study, look closely, examine. Notice details—is the bird a robin or a thrush? Is the stone quartz or granite? Details make the poem strong."

Alice Schertle says, "Images, sounds, feelings . . . a traffic jam, the taste of pizza, sand in my shoe. . . . The best inspiration of all, I think, is a SSN, a Sudden Strange Notion."

Joseph Bruchac says, "What inspires me to write a poem? It is this business of living, life itself."

J. Patrick Lewis says, "Ideas begin with words."

Poets, where will you try to get ideas today?

Book Links

These books can help you extend the minilesson.

Karla Kuskin
Near the Window Tree: Poems and Notes
HarperCollins (1975)

Paul Janeczko
The Place My Words Are Looking For: What Poets Say About and Through Their Work
Simon & Schuster (1990)

Paul Janeczko
Seeing the Blue Between: Advice and Inspiration for Young Poets
Candlewick (2002)

Listening for Songs from Our Hearts

Don't be afraid to sing your poems.
—Beverly McLoughland

I tell [children] that we are all poets, and that each of us has songs or rhymes or stories or word pictures that we can share. —Pat Mora

The children in your class now have the music and the magic of poetry inside them from listening to a variety of poems throughout the year. Poetry will now bloom in the hearts and minds of your students! Very young poets often compose their poems in their heads first, like little songs, speak them aloud and draw pictures, and then possibly write a few letters. We want to build on young children's foundation and comfort using oral language first as a connector to using written language. The following lesson is one way that I've found success in introducing poetry writing to very young poets and building on young children's oral language skills. From this lesson, children can learn that poems can be little songs from the heart and they can come from pictures in our minds.

After the minilesson, as children are composing their own poems and you are having one-on-one conversations with them, ask students to say or sing their poems to you. Write down their lovely songs and poems to help you (and them) remember the words of their poem.

Minilesson

Sometimes I think of poems as little songs from my heart. Poems are like little songs about what you love and care about in the world. A young poet just your age once sang a little poem about stars, and it went like this:

> Stars, stars
> They shine in the sky.
> They sparkle like
> they're brand new.

This poet loved stars—so he sang a little song about them, and then he drew a picture and wrote a few letters. I really like how this poet said that the stars were "like they're brand new." Does anyone know what this poet meant when he said that?

Another young poet sang this poem from her heart because she felt sad. Some of the butterflies in the classroom didn't hatch, and they died. She sang:

Angels sing
Hearts go away
Butterflies
Die

After she sang her poem to me, she wrote down a few letters on poetry paper so she would always remember her beautiful poem.

That's what poets do. They make up poems about whatever is on their hearts—sometimes happy poems and sometimes sad—say them out loud, draw pictures of their poems, and write down a few letters.

Today, you're going to be singing and saying your own poems from your hearts. I'd like everyone to close your eyes and picture something you love in the world. It could be stars in the night sky, someone in your family that you love—anything that you care about. You might want to rock back and forth, like when you listen to a song, and then sing your own song about something you love in the world.

Now sing your poem out loud to your partner. When you go back to your work spots, sing or say your poem, draw, and write a few letters from it.

Book Links

These books can help you extend the minilesson.

Jane Yolen
Here's A Little Poem: A Very First Book of Poetry
Candlewick (2007)

Eloise Greenfield
Honey, I Love and Other Love Poems
HarperTrophy (1986)

Arnold Adoff
Touch the Poem
Blue Sky Press (2000)

Jack Prelutsky, ed.
Read-Aloud Rhymes for the Very Young
Knopf (1986)

Karla Kuskin
Moon, Have You Met My Mother?
HarperCollins (2003)

Barbara Juster Esbensen
Swing Around the Sun: Poems
Lerner (2002)

Lilian Moore
I Feel the Same Way
Atheneum (1976)

Kristine O'Connell George
Little Dog Poems
Clarion Books (1999)

Mem Fox
Whoever You Are
Harcourt Children's Books (1997)

Seeing with Poets' Eyes

Pay attention to the world around you—little things, big things, people, animals, buildings . . . . What do you see, hear, taste, smell, feel? —Marilyn Singer

Sometimes children think they have nothing to write a poem about. They look at their life and see nothing with a label that says "this could be a poem." In this lesson, we try to help children see that poets aren't waiting to see something spectacular—they aren't waiting for a landslide or an eclipse to happen. Instead, poets can write about anything—anything, that is, that they've taken the time to truly see and be thoughtful about.

Minilesson

Poets, today I want to talk to you about how poets go about finding ideas for poems. When poets go for a walk or talk to their friends or do anything in the world, they always have their poets' eyes open. One young poet said, "When I look at anything, I can find a poem." Now, that's amazing. Has that ever happened to you? When you're walking to school, or looking out your window, do you ever notice something and say, "That could be a poem"? That happens to poets all the time. Poets have special eyes called poets' eyes, and we're always on the lookout for poems.

I'm remembering some of the poems that we've read this year together—do you remember, in "Laundromat," how X. J. Kennedy found poetry in doing the laundry? Another poet, Marilyn Singer, found poetry in making pretend soup! So, how do poets go about finding poems? Here's a list of some of what poets see with their poets' eyes.

Poets notice:

- the world around them
- small things
- their feelings and other people's feelings
- poems in unusual places
- beauty in places where a lot of people don't see it

Starting today, since we're all poets, I want everyone to change your eyes to poets' eyes. From now on, we're going to be walking around the world and noticing things that most people don't notice. Whenever we do this, you can take a piece of paper so you don't forget your ideas and can write them down. We'll have a little basket here for those special poems that you have found with your poets' eyes!

Extensions

- This is a good time to go for a "poetry walk." Go around the building; go outside; even go around the classroom to see what young poets can notice with their poets' eyes. Children might use a clipboard to help them write ideas as they walk. After the poetry walk, they could share the ideas as a class poem—either orally or as shared writing.
- In Mrs. Hig's second-grade class, young poets listed numerous ways they can go about finding poems within the classroom, especially if they have "poet's block" and don't know what to write about. Their ideas are printed below. See "Part One: Creating a Poetry-Rich Environment" for more about observation windows (Minilesson 7) and heartmaps (Minilesson 11).
  - We can go to the observation window and notice one thing outside that's interesting.
  - We can make a list of questions of what we wonder about.
  - We can go to the fish bowl and observe the fish.
  - We can close our eyes and create mind-pictures about something we've seen.
  - We can go inside our hearts and feel.
  - We can look in our poetry books to see what other poets have written about.
  - We can look at our heartmaps to see what really matters to us.

Book Links

These books can help you extend the minilesson.

Roni Schotter
Nothing Ever Happens on 90th Street
Scholastic (1999)

X. J. Kennedy
Elympics
Philomel (1999)

Kevin Henkes
All Alone
Greenwillow (2003)

Ralph Fletcher
Ordinary Things: Poems from a Walk in Early Spring
Atheneum (1997)

Valerie Worth
Peacock and Other Poems
Farrar, Straus and Giroux (2002)

Byrd Baylor
The Other Way To Listen
Aladdin (1997)

Nikki Giovanni
Spin a Soft Black Song: Poems for Children
Farrar, Straus and Giroux (1987)

Lilian Moore
Mural on Second Avenue and Other City Poems
Candlewick (2005)

Kristine O'Connell George
The Great Frog Race and Other Poems
Clarion Books (2005)

Finding Poems in Small, Ordinary Things

Sometimes I'll start writing a poem in bed. . . . Early in the morning the mind is still half-dreaming, swarming with vague, woozy thoughts, and some of those turn into poems. —X. J. Kennedy

One of our goals in teaching poetry is to guide young poets in learning that the seeds of poems are all around us and that a poet can write about anything no matter how small or ordinary. I frequently launch a poetry writing unit with this lesson because I want young poets to create an ongoing list of ideas for poems and to be truly inspired by this list (not a list that sits unused on a wall or in a notebook). From this lesson, children can learn:

- That poetry is all around them, even in the ordinary and small
- That one place where poetry hides can be the source for several poems
- To use oral language as a scaffold for drawing and writing
- To create an ongoing poetry topic list from which to write poems

On the list, write down students' words exactly as they say them. It's the unusual, not-perfect way of speaking that sometimes makes a thought more poetic.

Minilesson

Poetry hides all around us. Poetry sometimes hides in places where most people wouldn't think of looking, like under your bed, in a rain puddle on the street, or in a spider's web. Or sometimes poetry hides in ordinary places, like in a paper clip, a button, and even in a dog barking at a noisy vacuum cleaner—all of these are subjects for actual poems. Poetry is all around us if we just look for it. I'm going to read you part of a poem about where one poet found poetry.

Let's look at the poem, and pay particular attention to the lines in bold.

Valentine for Ernest Mann
By Naomi Shihab Nye
You can't order a poem like you order a taco.
Walk up to the counter, say, "I'll take two"
and expect it to be handed back to you
on a shiny plate.

Still, I like your spirit.
Anyone who says, "Here's my address,

write me a poem," deserves something in reply.
So I'll tell you a secret instead:
poems hide. In the bottoms of our shoes,
they are sleeping. They are the shadows
drifting across our ceilings the moment
before we wake up. What we have to do
is live in a way that lets us find them.

Once I knew a man who gave his wife
two skunks for a valentine.
He couldn't understand why she was crying.
"I thought they had such beautiful eyes."
And he was serious. He was a serious man
who lived in a serious way. Nothing was ugly
just because the world said so. He really
liked those skunks. So, he re-invented them
as valentines and they became beautiful.
At least, to him. And the poems that had been hiding
in the eyes of skunks for centuries
crawled out and curled up at his feet.

Maybe if we re-invent whatever our lives give us
we find poems. Check your garage, the odd sock
in your drawer, the person you almost like, but not quite.
And let me know.

Poems are sometimes hiding in places where people don't even think of looking. For me, poems hide in soapsuds, in my box of mints, and behind my son's ear! In one kindergarten class, the students illustrated a chart of where poetry hides for them. Here are some of the places where students found poetry hiding:

In leaves . . . (Jordon)
In the sound of rain on the roof . . . (Alex)
In a rainbow's pot of gold . . . (Daisy)
In the trees . . . (Leo)

Here are some other places where other young poets found poetry hiding. Let me read you two poems.

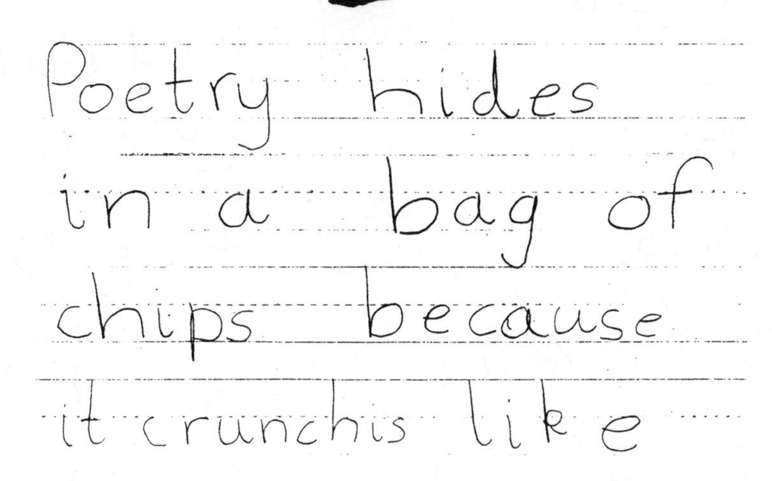

levs in the fall.
by Marissa
foran

Poetry hides
in a bag of
chips because
it crunches like
leaves in the fall.

Poetry hides
in music in the
Limmboe
Poetry hides
in your Shoe
whar it walks
Poetry hides
in a clock
in the humers
By Paul

Poetry hides
in a BaBBies
giggel
Poetry hides
in a spring
Picuoter.
By Paul

Poetry hides
in music in the
limbo
Poetry hides
in your shoe
when it walks
Poetry hides
in a clock
in the numbers

Poetry hides
in a baby's
giggle
Poetry hides
in a spring
picture

Why don't you close your eyes and think for a minute of where poetry hides for you. Now turn to someone next to you and whisper one place where you can find poetry. Who would like to share? As you tell me where you find poetry, I'll write it here on this Where Poetry Hides chart we'll keep in the classroom.

Extensions

- You can make a class book of places where poetry hides by collecting one idea from each student with their accompanying illustrations.
- Young poets can add the Where Poetry Hides list to their notebooks for ideas for future poems. Older children can check off one place that they might want to write more about.
- Be sure to point out that the Where Poetry Hides list is, in fact, a poem in itself, called a list poem.

Book Links

These books can help you extend the minilesson.

Karla Kuskin
Near the Window Tree: Poems and Notes
HarperCollins (1975)

Lee Bennett Hopkins
Good Books, Good Times!
Harper & Row (1990)

Paul Janeczko
The Place My Words Are Looking For: What Poets Say About and Through Their Work
Simon & Schuster (1990)

Paul Janeczko
Seeing the Blue Between: Advice and Inspiration for Young Poets
Candlewick (2002)

Finding Poems in Feelings

When you write poetry, you can express your joys and your sorrows. . . . Poetry writing helps you to share your feelings and to make yourself known in a new way.

—Patricia Hubbell

The foundation for most poems is the expression of feeling, which can come from a variety of sources: observations, memories, thoughts, and so on. In this minilesson, I address this fundamental inspiration of poetry and how to express our feelings using words. This lesson will help children learn that a feeling is a source for a poem and that describing where a feeling comes from is one way to develop a poem. You might ask pre-k and kindergarten poets to say their poems to a partner first, before going back to their work spots to write.

Minilesson

I want to talk to you today about another place where poetry comes from. Poems come from feelings that we have about our lives, the world, school, our families—really, anything. But it's not a poem if we just write our feelings down. For example, if I wanted to write a poem about how happy I feel today, I might write, "I am so happy. Happy. Happy. Today I am so happy." Would that sound like a poem? Not really!

Instead of just writing down my feeling, I will also try to describe what makes me feel so happy today. I might write something like this:

Today
I am
happy! [This is my feeling]
I get
to go
to the park
after school
and swing
on the swings. [And I think I'll end my poem with writing my feeling down again.]
Today
I am
happy!

When I show or tell you what's making me feel happy, then it's a poem. It's the same with all feelings: sadness, loneliness, or angriness. When you write about your feelings in your poems, be sure to show or tell us what's giving you that feeling.

I'd like to share with you two poems written by young poets where they show their feelings. The first one is about friendship:

Two Friends

Lydia and Shirley have
two pierced ears and
two bare ones.
Five pigtails
two pairs of sneakers
two smiles
one necklace
one bracelet
lots of stripes and
one good friendship

The second poem is just about feelings:

Philip

feelings

I'm sad my heart it feds, like a volcano erupting
exploding every miniute is beeps
when I have good feeling it feels like the sun
rising and there are no white cotin
in the way to block my feelings.

Feelings

I'm sad my heart it feels like a volcano erupting
exploding every minute is beeps
when I have good feeling it feels like the sun
rising and there are no white cotton
in the way to block my feelings.

Today, I'd like us to sit for a minute together, and try to think about how you're feeling today: happy, sad, angry, hurt, friendly, lonely, and so on. Let's be silent a moment and think about that.

Poets, when you go back to write your poems, be sure to tell us or show us how you feel and also what's making you feel that way.

Book Links

These books can help you extend the minilesson.

Eloise Greenfield
Honey, I Love and Other Love Poems
HarperTrophy (1986)

Nikki Grimes
Thanks a Million
Amistad (2006)

Georgia Heard
This Place I Know: Poems of Comfort
Candlewick (2002)

Joyce Carol Thomas
Crowning Glory
HarperCollins (2002)

Pat Mora
Love to Mamá: A Tribute to Mothers
Lee & Low Books (2001)

Georgia Heard
Songs of Myself: An Anthology of Poems and Art
Mondo (2000)

Lee Bennett Hopkins
Been to Yesterdays: Poems of a Life
Boyds Mills Press (1995)

Nikki Grimes
Shoe Magic
Scholastic (2000)

Donald Graves
Baseball, Snakes, And Summer Squash: Poems About Growing Up
Boyds Mills Press (1996)

Rebecca Kai Dotlich
Lemonade Sun: And Other Summer Poems
Boyds Mills Press (1998)

Jean Little
Hey World, Here I Am!
HarperTrophy (1990)

Finding Poems in Natural Beauty

So what is it that causes and creates poems for me?
It is the miraculous in the things of this world.

—Deborah Chandra

The beauty we observe in the world—stars, a maple tree on a city block, a pigeon crossing the street, snow falling, the sound of rain—begs to have poems written about it. Children don't have to live in a rural environment to notice the poetry in the world around them. I've seen nothing more beautiful than the early morning brilliantly lighting up my Manhattan street; I've seen nothing more inspiring than the shining rows of apples and oranges in the wooden crates at the corner deli. Poetry based on observation is sometimes easier to write than other kinds because observations can come in short bursts, unlike, for example, the time I first met my dog, which comes out more easily as a story, though it could be a poem.

Minilesson

Many poets write about the beautiful and amazing things they've seen in the world, like a night sky full of stars, a tree first budding in spring, or the sunlight shining on the red bricks of an apartment building. Sometimes the words in these poems give us such a clear picture in our minds that we feel like we're there, seeing it for ourselves.

I'm going to share a few poems written by poets your age—children who wrote poems about some of the inspiring things they saw in the world. I'd like you to close your eyes and picture the images of the poems as I read their words. That's one of the amazing things that poetry does—poetry words give us pictures in our minds.

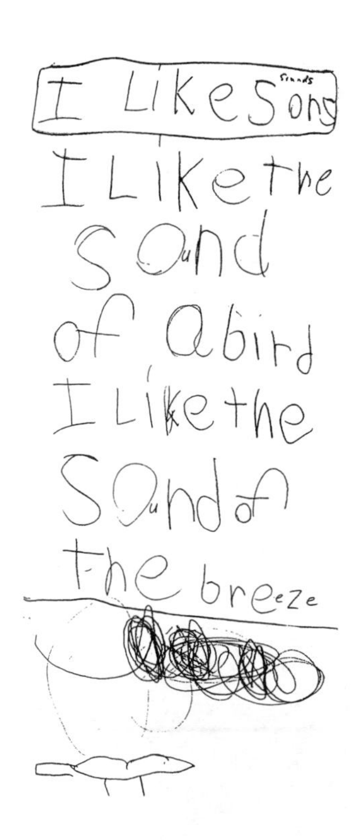

I Like Sounds
I like the sound
Of a bird
I like the
Sound of
The breeze

Ggpriel
Mon
tn emon
wllnevr
mak rhrt
sflat
ALVA

Moon
The moon is
Very beautiful
The moon
Will never
Make our hearts
Fall out

Spreeing
I sol the Birds
I sol the clous
Up in t heaer
The wind Bose
vareejtlee
(very gently)

Spring
I see the birds
I see the clouds
Up in the air
The wind blows
Very gently

I ~~blo~~
love
the
Sound
of
the
trees
rusling
in
the
air
they
are
So
Soft
and
lovely
Tust
wisaling
like
birds
the
eafs

blow
blow
blow
in
the
air
the
ladybirds
Crol
on
the
leafs
as
the
leafs
blow
in
the
air
the
leafs
~~leafs~~
love

the
bugs
ceeping
them
cumpany

I
love
the
sound
of
the
trees
rustling
in
the
air
they
are
so
soft
and
lovely

just
whistling
like
birds
the
leaves
blow
blow
blow
in
the
air
the
ladybirds
crawl
on
the

leaves
as
the
leaves
blow
in
the
air
the
leaves
love
the
bugs
keeping
them
company

Now that you've heard the poems, close your eyes, and try to picture something beautiful and amazing that you've seen outside that has stayed with you, like a tree on your block; a bird soaring in the sky; a certain cloud; or a huge, full moon. Remember, you can picture sounds, too, maybe the sound of rain or the silence of nighttime. Open your eyes, and whisper to the person next to you what you pictured in your mind.

Now that you've had a few minutes, will you two share what you saw in your minds so that we can all hear you?

Now, poets, please return to your seats to draw the picture and write the words of the picture you saw in your mind!

Extensions

- When students draw pictures to go with their poems, ask them to look back at the poem to see if the writing includes the details in the picture.
- Students could read their poems to a partner, and then ask the partner to draw a picture of the image the poem created in their minds. They might choose to revise their poems based on what their partners have seen.

Book Links

These books can help you extend the minilesson.

Tana Hoban
Look! Look! Look!
Greenwillow (1988)

Tana Hoban
Dots, Spots, Speckles, and Stripes
Greenwillow (1987)

Tana Hoban
Shapes, Shapes, Shapes
Greenwillow (1986)

Bruce McMillan
Fire Engine Shapes
Lothrop, Lee and Shepard (1988)

Thomas Locker
Sky Tree: Seeing Science Through Art
HarperCollins (1995)

Thomas Locker
Home: A Journey Through America
Silver Whistle Books (1998)

Valerie Worth
Peacock and Other Poems
Farrar, Straus and Giroux (2002)

Bobbi Katz
Once Around the Sun
Harcourt (2006)

Rebecca Kai Dotlich
Lemonade Sun: And Other Summer Poems
Boyds Mills Press (1998)

Carole Boston Weatherford
Sidewalk Chalk: Poems of the City
Boyds Mills Press (2001)

Kristine O'Connell George
Hummingbird Nest: A Journal of Poems
Harcourt (2004)

Lilian Moore
Mural on Second Avenue and Other City Poems
Candlewick (2005)

Modeling Writing

I think children can be very inventive in the right atmosphere that supports experimentation and offers praise, praise, praise. Few if any of the poets in this book would be published if all we'd received from teachers were corrections and negative comments. —Pat Mora

Modeling writing a poem in front of our students may seem scary, but it's one of the most powerful invitations for young poets to write their own poems. By thinking out loud and then writing our thoughts, we model the process of writing a poem. We can show our youngsters that writing is about experimentation and that poets try things and take risks! Be sure to keep your demonstration poem simple and short, and write about an everyday subject that you know your students can relate to: weather, a special food, a special person. This lesson will help children learn that the process of writing poems often involves:

- Writing from what you notice in the world
- Closing your eyes and seeing mind-pictures
- Rereading
- Carefully selecting words
- Adding more words

Minilesson

Yesterday afternoon I was looking up at the sky, and I noticed a bunch of huge, white clouds. I was in such a hurry that just looking at those clouds, drifting slowly across the sky, made me want to slow down. I thought to myself, "That could be a poem." I'm going to try writing my poem right here.

The first thing I'm going to do is to close my eyes and picture what I saw yesterday. Let's see . . . I see the clouds gliding across the sky. I'll start with writing the word "clouds."

I also want to describe to you how the clouds were moving in the sky. I'll write down the word "glide." I love the sound of that word. Clouds glide slowly, but instead of the word "slowly," I want to think of a more interesting, poetic word, so I'll change "slowly" to "lazily." Poets think carefully about their words, cross out weak or worn words, and replace them with more interesting words! Here's what I'll write:

Clouds
Glide
Lazily
Across
. . . Sky.

How about "a wide blue sky" instead of just the word "sky"? I'll reread what I have so far. Poets reread all the time. Hmmm. You know, poets, I could end my poem here, but I'm going to add a little bit more because I also want to tell you how I feel.

I'll skip a space here and write more words in a new stanza. Poets add words all the time when writing poetry!

Today, I wish
I could be
Slow and lazy
And drift
Like a cloud.

Poets, do you notice how I'm writing the poem long and thin, like other poems we've read, and not like a story? I think I'm finished. Will you help me read it back?

Poets, now it's your chance to write your own poems. Remember how I got my idea for my poem by thinking about something I noticed in the world. I'm going to give you a chance to think what you're going to write your poems about today. Close your eyes and see what ideas pop into your head.

Does anyone want to share? Does anyone already have the words of the poem in their minds? Let's hear from a few of you, and after you tell me your idea, I'll say it back to you so you can hear it too!

Now, poets, get pieces of poetry paper and get started writing your own poems.

Extensions

- You might want to write a shared poem with the class. You could start with a plain first line, like "Yesterday I saw . . ." Then ask children to close their eyes and make a mind-picture of something they saw. Offer an example of something your students could actually have seen, and use details as you describe it together. Write their words down in poetry form.
- After you've written your poem and children have brainstormed ideas for their poems, ask one or two poets to model writing their poems on chart paper in front of the class, as you did. Other suggestions for getting ideas for writing poetry can be found in "Part One: Creating a Poetry-Rich Environment."

SECTION 2
Craft

Now that children have started writing and speaking their poems in the poetry writing workshop, and you've given them strategies for getting ideas and beginning to write their own poems, take a minute to stand back and assess the workshop and children's poems. Assessing the workshop at this midpoint will guide you in proceeding through the next section about teaching the crafting of poetry.

Here are some points to focus on, as you assess your students:

- Are the children able to choose their own topics?
- Do children's poems make sense, or are they burdened by awkward rhymes?
- Are children's poems poem-like, or are they story-like?
- Are children's poems lively?

Suggestions follow for assessing and addressing each of these questions. You will also find minilessons for teaching poetry-crafting tools.

Are the children able to choose their own topics?

- When children have "poet's block," refer them to the Observation Window, Poetry Museum, or Poetry Place in your classroom, so they can help themselves find an idea for a poem. (See "Part One: Creating a Poetry-Rich Environment"; Minilessons 7, 8, and 10.)
- After each minilesson, you might have children speak, or even sing, their poems to their partners. Speaking a poem before writing it will build on young children's natural strength with oral language and use that as a connector to written language.
- After the minilesson, as a way to find out if there are any poets who don't have ideas for their poems, you might gently place the palm of your hand on the top of children's heads, in turn, and ask them to quickly tell you what their poem will be about today before sending them off to write. If they don't know, you might say:
  - "You know a lot about ______ (a topic you're studying in class or that they're an expert about). You could write a poem about that."
  - "How about writing about something you love in nature: the stars, frogs, bumblebees, butterflies, ocean waves, wind, rain, trees . . .?"
  - "How about writing about your friends? Make a list of what you like about them and what you like to do with them."

- "Why don't you go over to the Observation Window or the Poetry Museum and write a poem about what you observe." (See above.)
- "You could read ideas from the Where Poems Hide chart." (Minilesson 5.)

Do children's poems make sense, or are they burdened by awkward rhymes?

Example of a line burdened by rhyme: "The moon is a spoon."

Always celebrate the poem children write first, and ask them what made them write about this idea today. If it's a topic that matters to them (and not just an idea that popped into their minds because of the rhyming words), ask them to close their eyes and picture whatever they're writing about. Ask them to tell you what they see in their minds. Write down what they tell you, and when they open their eyes, read it back to them.

You might say, "You can get a second piece of poetry paper and do what poets do all the time—after a poet writes one poem about a topic, she sometimes realizes there is more to say, so she writes another poem about the same idea. So this time when you close your eyes, try getting mind-pictures first before writing your next poem, and don't even try to rhyme."

Are children's poems poem-like, or are they story-like?

Example of a story-like line: "One day I went to the beach and I was walking on the beach with my sister and we were walking with my dog on the beach. . . ."

In this situation, you might read the poem back to the poet and ask, "What do you think—does it sound more like a poem or a story? I'd like you to close your eyes and create a mind-picture. Tell me what you see. What's the first thing you see in your mind when you picture that? Here's a new piece of poetry paper. Try making a poem by writing just what you see, hear, and feel in your mind-picture."

Are children's poems lively?

Example of a flat poetic line: "Snow is nice. I like snow."

Again, encouraging poets to use imagery or mind-pictures can be helpful here. You can give a minilesson on metaphor and simile, or suggest adding a surprise to the poem. You might ask the child to describe the topic in a way no one else has ever done before: "I'm going to ask you to picture this in your mind. What do you picture?

Do you hear anything? Here's a new piece of paper—why don't you try writing what you picture in your mind on this new piece of paper? Once you have two poems about the same subject, I'm going to read both poems back to you. Which one expresses more of what you wanted to say?"

Teaching Poetry-Crafting Tools

Teaching the craft of poetry writing doesn't have to be complicated. It's helpful to remember, when we teach our students the tools and craft of poetry, that craft is always at the service of the heart. In other words, the reason why poets know and use such tools as, for example, alliteration and imagery, is to better express what's in our hearts. The point is not to teach the labels of the tools but, instead, to teach how the tools help young poets express themselves in more vivid and accurate ways. Function precedes form.

We teach five ways of crafting poetry:

- metaphor and simile
- word choice
- imagery
- music: rhyme, rhythm, and repetition
- lines and stanzas

Each of these lessons will be short but should be re-taught or supported not just once but several times.

Metaphor and Simile: "The sky is an angel's pool."

Poetry gives the reader the 'ah-ha' experience, by which he will look at something now in a way he had never thought to do before. —J. Patrick Lewis

But I can't leave out the power of metaphor. There is hardly a time I don't look at a dandelion or an empty bird nest, a turtle shell or a marble and compare it to something else. —Deborah Chandra

Poetry lets us see things in new ways and sometimes finds the one unexpected way that very different things are alike. —Bobbi Katz

We hear young children speaking metaphors and similes all day long in the classroom. One first-grader described the sky as being "an angel's pool" instead of "blue." Poetry helps us look at the world in a new way and describe it like no one has before, and that's one of the functions of metaphor and simile.

It's not as important to teach young children the terms "metaphor" and "simile" as it is to discuss what metaphor and simile can do. I tell young poets that a poem should surprise us by describing something we see every day in a new way. Later on, you might want to teach young poets the distinction between metaphor and simile, but at first just let them practice making and recognizing metaphor and simile. This lesson can help students learn to reach beyond their first words to find new ways to describe ordinary things.

Minilesson

I know a poet who wrote a beautiful poem about a paper clip—a little paper clip just like this one. It's amazing how she was able to find poetry hiding inside a paper clip. It's easy to find it in the moon, or the stars, but in a paper clip—that's difficult! Before I read this paper clip poem to you, let's try to find some poetry inside a paper clip ourselves.

Let's try something: I have a T-chart here with the word "Ordinary" on the left side and the word "Poetry" on the right. First, what are the first words that come to mind when you look at this paper clip? Silver? Shiny? I'm going to write whatever you say under the word "Ordinary." Now that we've collected those words, let's reread them together. Does this sound like a poem? I don't think it does either!

If we were going to write a poem about a paper clip, how could we describe it in unusual and surprising ways? For example, under the word "Poetry" I might write, "shiny as a star in the night sky." What are some of your ideas? Some other children have said:

The paper clip
Shaped like a boat.
Looks
like a small fish.

Let's reread what you've said. Now that is sounding like poetry! Next, I'm going to read you Rebecca Kai Dotlich's poem "Paper Clips." As I read, look at the paper clip and listen carefully for all the surprising ways she describes it.

Paper Clips

By Rebecca Kai Dotlich

With tiny teeth
of tin
they take
one slender breath
before they make
a move,
and then—
a silver pinch!

With jaws
no bigger
than an inch
these dragon grips
are small and slight—
but
conquer pages
with
one
bite!

Amazing, isn't it, to find poetry in a paper clip? Today we're going to write a poem together about an object we use every day in the classroom. Does anyone have any ideas what object we might write about?

A stapler? A pencil? Let's choose a pencil, and I'm going to write down what we think of. "A pencil is like . . ." How many unusual, surprising ways can we describe a pencil? After we do this poem together, you can go back to your work spots and write your own poem about an everyday object.

Extensions

- Young poets might be inspired to write other poems using similes and metaphors after reading the children's poetry in the following poems.

Corn

Corn
Oh
Corn
It looks
Like
Teeth
Falling
Out

Flowers

The
Flowers
Are
The
Sun's
Children

Mom by Bobby
You're like a rose.
When you scold me
I feel your thorns.
When you smile
you're like the red petals.
When you cry
it's like a crystal dropping
off your leaf.

Emma
back and fourth
Zippity Zip
It bangs along it's little rail
like a tiny engine
along a railroad trail
zippity zip
up my coat
it fastens on
open and close
that the way
my zipper goes

Mom

You're like a rose.
When you scold me
I feel your thorns.
When you smile
You're like the red petals.
When you cry
It's like a crystal dropping
Off your leaf.

Zipper

Back and forth
Zippity zip
It bangs along its little rail
Like a tiny engine
Along a railroad trail
Zippity zip
Up my coat
It fastens on
Open and close
That's the way
My zipper goes

Book Links

These books can help you extend the minilesson.

Loreen Leedy
There's a Frog in My Throat: 440 Animal Sayings a Little Bird Told Me
Holiday House (2003)

Cynthia Rylant
In November
Harcourt (2000)

Lester Laminack
Saturdays and Teacakes
Peachtree (2004)

Reeve Lindbergh
Grandfather's Lovesong
Viking (1993)

Brenda Seabrooke
Looking for Diamonds
Dutton (1995)

Marion Dane Bauer
When I Go Camping with Grandma
Clarion (1995)

Patricia MacLachlan
All the Places to Love
Joanna Colter (1994)

Lenore Look
Love as Strong as Ginger
Atheneum (1999)

Jan Greenburg
Heart to Heart: New Poems Inspired by Twentieth-Century American Art
Harry N. Abrams (2001)

David Miller
Just Like You and Me
Dial (2001)

Lee Bennett Hopkins
School Supplies: A Book of Poems
Simon & Schuster (1996)

Valerie Worth
All the Small Poems and Fourteen More
Farrar, Straus and Giroux (1994)

Deborah Chandra
Rich Lizard: And Other Poems
Farrar, Straus and Giroux (1993)

Deborah Chandra
Balloons: And Other Poems
Farrar, Straus and Giroux (1990)

Rebecca Kai Dotlich
Lemonade Sun: And Other Summer Poems
Boyds Mills Press (1998)

Wonderful Words: "Let the rain kiss you."

Each poem written is a package of words.
—Rebecca Kai Dotlich

A painter uses paint to create a painting, and a poet uses words to create a poem. And both a painting and a poem can help us to create an image, to see new things in our minds. Words are a poet's tool. Since many poems are short, it's essential that words in a poem be vivid and alive. Choosing words that will make a poem sing is a large part of creating a poem. Introducing this lesson to young poets will help their words fly. Through this lesson, they can learn to select unique, precise, and interesting words when they write poems.

Minilesson

Because many poems are so short, and it doesn't take long to read a poem, poets must choose their words very carefully. Words in a poem are kind of like magic—words that are carefully chosen can make us feel or see the poem. Listen to some of these unusual words that poets have used in their poems!

The poet Langston Hughes wrote about April rain in his poem "April Rain Song." Listen to this. He wrote, "Let the rain *kiss* you." He could have written, "Let the rain *drip* on your head," but he wanted to use a word that was more surprising, I think, so he chose "kiss." You can almost feel the soft rain falling on his face like little cat kisses.

And listen to this poem written by a young poet: "When I run / I feel the wind / *bloom* on my face." "Bloom!" What an interesting word! He could have written, "When I run / I feel the wind / *blow* on my face." But that would have been boring, so he chose "bloom" instead.

Here are a two more examples from kids who use amazing words in their poems:

Clouds

Clouds swishing
Clouds going
Clouds smashing
Clouds thumping
Clouds bumping
Clouds clipping and dipping
Clouds rumbling
Clouds flipping

Shadows in the Air

Shadows in the air
Swiffling all over my
Wall onto my lap
Like a horse jumping

When you write your poems today, choose your words carefully. Choose words that are just right, words that are unusual—poetic words. And when we come back to our share time, we'll share some of these wonderful words that you've included in your poems.

Extensions

- With older poets, you might want to explore a specific part of speech such as verbs or nouns. I usually begin with a verb study since strong verbs can transform a poem from a static poem with no energy to a lively and energized poem. I demonstrate the differences that lively verbs make in the following two versions of "The Pencil Sharpener" from my book *The Revision Toolbox: Teaching Techniques that Work*. In the first version, I use weak verbs; in the second version, I have substituted stronger verbs. Invite students to compare and contrast the versions.

Version 1:	*Version 2:*
The pencil sharpener **makes** the pencil into a sharp point and **leaves** the leftovers out.	The pencil sharpener **chews** the pencil into a sharp point and **spits** the leftovers out.

- Find "Night Story" by Beverly McLoughland in the *Climb Inside a Poem* big book (p. 35). Read aloud lines 1–5: "When the blue page of day / is turned to night, / An alphabet of stars / Is printed, small and bright, / On dark and ancient-storied skies." Ask your students what interesting, strong, magical words they hear in this poem.
- For pre-k and kindergarten poets, you might change the minilesson a bit by asking children about their favorite words: "Which words do you just love to say? A poet just your age told me her favorite word is 'galoshes.' Let's say it together. Aren't the sounds wonderful? Turn to the person next to you and say your favorite-sounding words. Poets, when you're making your poems, remember to use words you love!"

Book Links

These books can help you extend the minilesson.

Arnold Adoff
Touch the Poem
Blue Sky Press (2000)

Paul Paolilli and Dan Brewer
Silver Seeds: A Book of Nature Poems
Viking (2001)

George Shannon
Frog Legs: A Picture Book of Action Verse
Greenwillow (2000)

Roni Schotter
The Boy Who Loved Words
Schwartz & Wade (2006)

J. Patrick Lewis
Please Bury Me in the Library
Gulliver Books (2005)

Lee Bennett Hopkins
Wonderful Words: Poems About Reading, Writing, Speaking, and Listening
Simon & Schuster (2004)

Barbara Juster Esbensen
Words with Wrinkled Knees: Animal Poems
Boyds Mills Press (1998)

Beverly McLoughland
A Hippo's a Heap: And Other Animal Poems
Boyds Mills Press (1993)

Imagery: "Do you feel the golden glow?"

I suppose that I could say my poems often start with pictures . . . pictures only I can see. —Janet Wong

One absolutely perfect June morning, I went for a walk before work. What if I could preserve that day, the way my mom had preserved raspberries by cooking them and sealing them in jars? Then I could share a taste of summer on the most shivery day of winter. —Bobbi Katz

I can close my eyes and remember the smell of my grandfather's dirt-floor garage . . . I can hear the coins jingling in my father's pocket . . . I can still feel how it felt to dance on my father's feet or the wind in my hair when I rode my bike. —Rebecca Kai Dotlich

You might introduce this lesson by reading aloud the picture book *Frederick*, by Leo Lionni, and then circling back to excerpts from the book for the minilesson. In the story, Frederick the mouse stores the beautiful, colorful mind-pictures of summer in his mind for a cold, dreary, gray winter day. That's what poets do—they store pictures in their minds and then write about those stored pictures. The ability to create mind-pictures, or imagery, is a quality of good writing that runs through every genre from poetry to picture books to nonfiction books. In this lesson, children learn that mind-pictures can inspire poets to write and can help poets use vivid words and details.

Minilesson

Poets, today I'm going to share with you part of one of my favorite books: *Frederick* by Leo Lionni. It's about a little mouse named Frederick who sits there doing nothing while all the other mice are gathering food for the cold winter. The other mice ask him, "Frederick, why don't you work?" Frederick says, "I do work, I gather sun rays for the cold dark winter days." When the mice ask him again, "Frederick, why don't you work?" Frederick says, "I gather colors . . . for winter is gray."

Frederick is a poet, and his work has been storing all the beautiful mind-pictures and colors in his mind, such as the color of the berries and the warm feel of the sun. When the cold winter comes, and the food is gone, Frederick says to the other mice, "Close your eyes. Now I send you the rays of the sun. / Do you feel . . . their golden glow?" As Frederick speaks, the cold mice begin to feel warmer.

How does Frederick do this? Mind-pictures! They can make four cold mice feel warm again even in the middle of winter.

Okay, Fredericks! I'd like you to make mind-pictures of something you've stored in your minds. It could be sunlight on the trees, wind blowing leaves, or clouds moving across the sky. . . . We all have mind-pictures of things we love or have seen stored in our minds, like Frederick. I have an example from a poet your age to share.

SORZe ShIn
SORZe tweG
In My
HRte Your
RaLey UP
HIVe You
Shin Like
The Moon

Stars Shining
Stars twinkle
In my
Heart you're
Really up
High you
Shine like
The moon

When you write your poems, you can write about your mind-pictures. Now close your eyes, and whisper to the person next to you what you see in your mind. Then open your eyes, tiptoe back to your seats, and draw pictures and write words from what you see in your minds.

Extensions

- Another way to show students that the words in a poem can give them mind-pictures is by inviting them to illustrate a poem. Select a poem that contains images or mind-pictures (see Book Links). Have blank white paper, colored markers and pencils, and even watercolors available. After reading a poem aloud, ask students to draw a picture of what the words make them see in their minds. If it's a long poem with several images, ask students to illustrate particular lines or stanzas to create a class picture book.
- Students can begin to reflect on the mind-pictures in their own poems by drawing on paper the pictures in their minds and then comparing the written image with the drawn image. They can see if there are any details they left out of their poems that appeared in their drawing paper.

Book Links

These books can help you extend the minilesson.

Leo Lionni
Frederick
Knopf (1967)

Ed Young
Seven Blind Mice
Philomel (1992)

Cynthia Rylant
Night in the Country
Atheneum (1986)

Aileen Fisher
Always Wondering: Some Favorite Poems of Aileen Fisher
HarperCollins (1991)

Alice Schertle
A Lucky Thing
Harcourt (1999)

Janet Wong
Night Garden: Poems from the World of Dreams
Margaret K. McElderry (2000)

Rhythm, Repetition, and Rhyme: Musical Tools

Notice the rhythm of the words and the patterns of the lines. . . . You'll develop an ear for the sounds and rhythm of language almost like developing an ear for music.

—Alice Schertle

Poems can make us dance, clap our hands, and snap our fingers, just like songs. Music in a poem is a kind of glue that holds a poem together. There are many different kinds of musical tools in poetry: rhyme, rhythm, and repetition, to name a few. When children hear a rhythmic poem, they want to clap their hands and sway back and forth to the rhythm. Children are delighted by the playfulness and musicality of poems that rhyme and use word patterns.

Minilesson on Rhythm

Sometimes, when I hear a poem, I want to clap my hands or snap my fingers to the beat of the poem. It's like a little song that has a rhythm or a beat. Some poems have more music than others. I'm going to read you a poem that has a lot of music in it. You can clap your hands to the beat or snap your fingers as I read it. It's called "How I Hopscotch" by Kristine O'Connell George (*Climb Inside a Poem* big book, p. 13).

It's amazing that this poem has a rhythm like a song that we could actually dance to if we wanted. Today as you're writing your poems, I want you to see if you can make your poem have a beat or a rhythm. See if you can get us to clap our hands when you share your poem. Tap your fingers as you write your poem!

Minilesson on Repetition

Some poems sound like little songs, and one way that poems are like little songs is that they repeat words. Listen to this poem, "Happy Toes" by Pat Mora (*Climb Inside a Poem* big book, p. 5). Do you hear the words the poet says over and over? She says "chase our toes" two times, and then at the end of the poem she changes it a little bit to say, "chasing, chasing, tickles / our happy toes." Poets say words over again because it makes the poem like a song. Here are two more poems written by young poets just your age who repeated words:

Brs are singing in a chrey
I her ~~the~~ them in the moning
Brs are singing in a chrey
I her them singing to me
Brs are singing in a chrey
I her them singingto me
I sing bac to them Brs are
singing in a thees Madison

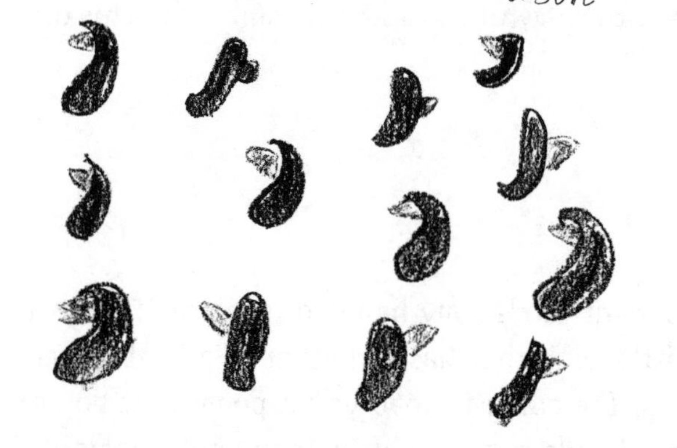

Sno foling sno foling
all wrld arad the
sno foling sno foling
all wrld arad the
the sno and
the wind our doing
A lalbiy

Birds
Birds are singing in a tree
I hear them in the morning
Birds are singing in a tree
I hear them singing to me
Birds are singing in a tree
I hear them singing to me
I sing back to them
Birds are singing in the trees

Snow
Snow falling snow falling
All around the world

Snow falling snow falling
All around the world

The snow and
The wind are doing
A lullaby

Today, when you write your poems, I'd like you to try making a little song by using repeating words and lines.

Minilesson on Rhyme

Now that we've listened to a lot of poems, we know that sometimes poems rhyme and sometimes they don't. We've listened to poems that don't rhyme and poems that do rhyme. But not every word in a poem has to rhyme. It's usually the last word in the line that *rhymes*. I'm going to read this poem that *rhymes*: "Song for My Swing" by Patricia Hubbell (*Climb Inside a Poem* big book, p. 19). Listen for the words that rhyme. Do you hear which words rhyme—*high/sky, grass/pass, air/hair, space/place*?

Today, when you write your poems, try adding rhymes—but make sure that the rhymes in the poem make sense!

Book Links

These books can help you extend the minilesson.

Rhythm:

Marc Brown
Hand Rhymes
Dutton (1985)

Eric Carle
Today Is Monday
Philomel (1993)

Leo Dillon and Diane Dillon
Rap A Tap Tap: Here's Bojangles—Think of That!
Blue Sky Press (2002)

Mem Fox
Time for Bed
Gulliver Books (1993)

Mem Fox
The Magic Hat
Harcourt (2002)

Bill Martin, Jr. and John Archambault
Chicka Chicka Boom Boom
Simon & Schuster (1989)

Steve Webb
Tanka Tanka Skunk!
Orchard Books (2004)

Repetition:

Michael Dennis Brown
Give Her the River: A Father's Wish for His Daughter
Atheneum (2004)

Leo Dillon and Diane Dillon
Rap A Tap Tap: Here's Bojangles—Think of That!
Blue Sky Press (2002)

Cynthia Rylant
In November
Harcourt (2000)

Barbara Seuling
Whose House?
Gulliver Books (2004)

Margaret Wild
Our Granny
Houghton Mifflin (1994)

Beverly McLoughland
A Hippo's a Heap: And Other Animal Poems
Boyds Mills Press (1993). See "Song of the Polar Bear."

J. Patrick Lewis
Big Is Big (and little, little): A Book of Contrasts
Holiday House (2007)

David McCord
Every Time I Climb a Tree
Little, Brown (1999)

Margaret Wise Brown
Nibble Nibble
HarperCollins (1998)

Dee Lillegard
Go: Poetry in Motion
Knopf (2006)

Langston Hughes
The Dreamkeeper and Other Poems
Knopf (1996)

Rhyme:

Marc Brown
Hand Rhymes
Dutton (1985)

Rebecca Kai Dotlich
When Riddles Come Rumbling: Poems to Ponder
Boyds Mills Press (2001)

David L. Harrison
Farmer's Garden: Rhymes for Two Voices
Boyds Mills Press (2000)

Jack Prelutsky
Read a Rhyme, Write a Rhyme
Knopf (2005)

Barbara Seuling
Whose House?
Gulliver Books (2004)

Eileen Spinelli
Feathers: Poems About Birds
Henry Holt and Co. (2004)

Rebecca Kai Dotlich
Over in the Pink House: New Jump-Rope Rhymes
Boyds Mills Press (2004)

Karla Kuskin
Near the Window Tree: Poems and Notes
HarperCollins (1975)

David McCord
Every Time I Climb a Tree
Little, Brown (1999)

Douglas Florian
Comets, Stars, the Moon, and Mars: Space Poems and Paintings
Harcourt (2007)

Marilyn Singer
Creature Carnival
Hyperion (2004)

J. Patrick Lewis
Big Is Big (and little, little): A Book of Contrasts
Holiday House (2007)

Lines and Stanzas: "Poems are shaped like tall buildings."

I can imagine the way the poem will look on the page.
—Rebecca Kai Dotlich

The fun part [is] . . . shaping the poem to give it an interesting look on the page. —Patricia Hubbell

An important difference between a story and a poem is that poems use lines and stanzas, while stories use sentences and paragraphs. A line break indicates how the poet wants the poem to be read. For young poets, pre-k through first grade, it works well to introduce the line break by talking about how the poem looks on the page. You could also talk with children about how line breaks affect the way the poem sounds. That approach works especially well with older students.

Minilesson

Today I want to show you something interesting about poetry, and something you may have noticed before. Did you ever notice that poems look different from stories? I've brought a picture book, and I want us to compare the pages to a poem, "Birthday Candles" by Rebecca Kai Dotlich (*Climb Inside a Poem* big book, p. 18). Look at this poem, and look at this story. See how poems are tall and skinny and look like tall buildings? Stories are written all the way across the page like this. Poems have shorter lines, and they even sometimes have one word on a line, like the first line of "Birthday Candles." Today, when you write your poems, remember to put a few words or even one word on a line when you write.

Extensions

- Practice reading poems together, pointing at the words on one line and pausing before reading the following line. (See "Supporting Children in Reading Aloud," in "Part Two: Reading Poetry.")
- Stanza Breaks: The word "stanza" means "room" in Italian. I teach young poets that if they want to have several rooms in their "poetry house," they can skip a line and then write their next "room of words"—their next stanza.

Book Links

These books can help you extend the minilesson.

Arnold Adoff
Touch the Poem
Blue Sky Press (2000)

Paul Paolilli and Dan Brewer
Silver Seeds
Viking (2001)

Eileen Spinelli
Feathers: Poems About Birds
Henry Holt (2004)

Marc Brown
Hand Rhymes
Dutton (1985)

Rebecca Kai Dotlich
When Riddles Come Rumbling: Poems to Ponder
Boyds Mills Press (2001)

Eloise Greenfield
In the Land of Words: New and Selected Poems
Amistad (2004)

David L. Harrison
Farmer's Garden: Rhymes for Two Voices
Boyds Mills Press (2000)

Lee Bennett Hopkins
Home to Me: Poems Across America
Orchard (2002)

Patricia Hubbell
City Kids: Poems
Marshall Cavendish Corporation (2001)

J. Patrick Lewis
Monumental Verses
National Geographic Children's Books (2005)

J. Patrick Lewis
Doodle Dandies: Poems That Take Shape
Aladdin (2002)

Cynthia Rylant
Waiting to Waltz: A Childhood
Atheneum/Richard Jackson Books (2001)

SECTION 3
New Forms

Three types of form poetry make it into most elementary school classrooms: haiku, cinquain, and diamante. They are included in almost every book on teaching poetry. I've included four other types of poems that I've had wonderful success teaching to younger poets:

- Poems for Two Voices
- List Poems
- Personification Poems
- Letter Poems

Poems for Two Voices

Poetry matters for many reasons. It is the language of the heart and the spirit. —Joseph Bruchac

Poems for two voices are written to be read aloud by two readers at once, the first reader reading the left-hand part of the poem, the second reader reading the right-hand part. When the words are on the same line (left-hand and right-hand side), across from one another, they are to be read together. It works well to write a two-voiced poem using a content-area topic, such as animals, because children can integrate their knowledge of a subject into their poems. Of course, the two voices can also represent two kinds of language coming from the same mind—a very common state for the heart and spirit!

Minilesson

Today we're going to be writing a very special kind of poem, called a Poem for Two Voices. This kind of poem is meant to be read aloud not just by one person but by two.

Let's start by reading this poem I've put on chart paper, "Frog Serenade" by Georgia Heard. As you can see, the poem is written in two columns: the words on the left side are read by one person, and the words on the right side are read by a different person. When the words are on the same line, across from one another, the two readers read the words together. Georgia Heard has said that when she was listening to frogs singing at a pond one evening, they didn't say "Ribbit" but said "Ga-lunk" instead. So, as we read this poem, you'll be the frogs and say "Ga-lunk, Ga-lunk," and I'll say the words on the other side of the poem.

Let's practice first. Let's all say "Ga-lunk," deep from the back of our throats. Okay, when I point to the word "Ga-lunk" in the poem, you'll say that, and when I point to the words on the other side of the poem, then I'll say those words. Ready, frogs?

Frog Serenade

A poem for two voices

By Georgia Heard from *Creatures of Earth, Sea, and Sky*

Ga-lunk

Ga-lunk

Ga-lunk	
	I hear your
Ga-lunk	
	deep-voiced songs
Ga-lunk	
Ga-lunk	
Ga-lunk	
	by the pond
Ga-lunk	
	this warm
	summer
	night.
Ga-lunk	
Ga-lunk	
Ga-lunk	
	I hear your
Ga-lunk	
	chorus of
Ga-lunk	
Ga-lunk	
Ga-lunk	
	banjo songs
Ga-lunk	
	under the shining stars
	tonight.

Today I thought that we could practice writing a poem for two voices about an animal that you know a lot about. I'll write the name of an animal at the top of this chart paper. Down the left side, let's write what sound the animal makes. I'm going to write the animal sound three times, then skip a space and write it three more times, and then skip another space and write it the last three times. Down the right side, let's write some facts about the animal—what do you know about this animal? I'll write the facts you give me on the right-hand side of the chart paper, where there are no animal sounds. Now let's read it together!

Let's go back to our work spots and try writing some poems for two voices on our own. We'll read them together in a while.

owls flying by

hooo
hooo
hooo

owls soud
like gost

hooo
hooo
hooo

owls can
scar cros

hooo
hooo

I here you
in the nhigt.
And hunting
for your
pray.

hoooo
hoooo
hoooo

hoooo
hoooo
hoooo

Owls

Owls flying by

Hoo
Hoo
Hoo

Owls sound like
Ghosts

Hoo
Hoo
Hoo

Owls can
Scare crows

Hoo
Hoo

I hear you
In the night
Hunting
For your — Hoo
Prey — Hoo
Hoo

Ladybugs

2 voices

Ladybugs are spotted	
	I am caught in a jar
I like my spots	I like my spots
I can't fly now	
	I'm in a jar
Lady bugs are spotted	Lady bugs are spotted

Extension

- After students have done some research on a particular animal (or another topic), you could invite them to write a poem for two voices based on what they have learned. You might ask them to brainstorm traits of their animals, using a web or other graphic organizer. You could also offer some questions to prompt their thoughts:
  - What does your animal look like? Sound like? (Be specific. Not "furry" but "fur: soft and spotted, black and white.")
  - Where does it live? (On a mountain cliff? In a warm ocean?)
  - What is it doing? (Slithering along the desert floor?)
  - What does it eat?
  - What's special about it? What do you wonder?

  Children can use their notes to help them write. They can ask themselves more questions. Which words should the readers say at the same time?

Book Links

These books can help you extend the minilesson.

David L. Harrison
Farmer's Garden: Rhymes for Two Voices
Boyds Mills Press (2000)

David L. Harrison
Farmer's Dog Goes to the Forest: Rhymes for Two Voices
Boyds Mills Press (2005)

Eloise Greenfield
The Friendly Four
Amistad (2006)

Mary Ann Hobermann
You Read to Me, I'll Read to You: Very Short Stories to Read Together
Little, Brown Young Readers (2001)

Paul Fleischman
Joyful Noise: Poems for Two Voices
Laura Geringer (1998)

Paul Fleischman
I Am Phoenix: Poems for Two Voices
HarperTrophy (1989)

J. Patrick Lewis
A World of Wonders: Geographic Travels in Verse and Rhyme
Dial (2002). See "Two Animals Talking."

List Poems

A poem doesn't fall onto the page, you have to put it there, word by word. —Rebecca Kai Dotlich

The list poem is one of the easiest and most successful types of poems for young children to write. Why? Because the list poem format is short, simple, familiar (everybody makes lists) and, most importantly, children feel successful when they try writing a list poem themselves. Building on young poets' strength with oral language, we begin by practicing a list poem out loud, and eventually children will write one on their own.

Minilesson

Poets, today we're going to be writing a poem together called a list poem. Does anyone have any idea what a list poem is? A list poem is a list but with an ending. There are two list poems in our big book: "Why? Why? Why?" by Lee Bennett Hopkins and "How I Hopscotch" by Kristine O'Connell George (*Climb Inside a Poem* big book, p. 9, p. 13).

Here are two examples of list poems written by students.

Hagre
By Danyel Gaddes
hagre [illegible]
stmics
groling
coling ing
for fod

Hungry
Hungry
Stomachs
Growling
Calling
For food

Speace
Dark
lonley
Black
Woods
Peaceful
Cold
Night
Brave
Scared

Space
Dark
Lonely
Black
Woods
Peaceful
Cold
Night
Brave
Scared

Now, let's think of something we could write a list poem about, something that you are interested in or connects with your lives. Hmmm . . . Dinosaurs? Balloons? Thanksgiving? Let's pick something. Okay, now I'd like everyone to close your eyes, and think about the topic we picked and come up with one word about it. Share your one word with the person next to you.

I'm writing our topic on the chart paper. When it's your turn, just say the word you thought of, and I'll write it down. If someone has already said your word, that's okay, because poems often have repeating words. Ready? Go!

Wow! What a list! Now, let's come up with an ending. A new word might sum it all up, or we can repeat an important word to end. Any ideas?

Today, try writing a list poem independently during work time.

Book Links

These books can help you extend the minilesson.

Anna Currey
I Want Another Little Brother: Poems About Families
Puffin (1999). See "Salty Sea" by Carl Saville (age 5).

Douglas Florian
Lizards, Frogs, and Polliwogs
Harcourt (2001). See "The Newt" and "The Bullfrog."

George Shannon
Busy in the Garden
Greenwillow (2006). See "Dig In," "Badminton, Bad!," "Luck," "A Corny Recipe," and "Grass."

Carol Diggory Shields
Almost Late to School: And More School Poems
Dutton (2003). See "Oral Report" and "B-Ball."

Georgia Heard
Falling Down the Page: List Poems
Roaring Brook Press (2008)

Personification Poems

A good poem . . . uses words wonderfully, and it uses them to capture specific moments in a fresh way, a way that makes the reader exclaim with delight, "Yes, that's it! That's right!" —Marilyn Singer

Children already use personification (attributing human qualities to something non-human) in their day-to-day lives. They turn trees into friends; they make friends with ladybugs—a child's world is personified. Exploring personification with children is fun and easy because it's a natural way that children view the world.

Many poems use personification. I love "Sun and Moon: A Poem for Two Voices" by Bobbi Katz (*Climb Inside a Poem* big book, pp. 30–31).

Minilesson

In this poem I'm going to read to you, "Sun and Moon: A Poem for Two Voices," the poet is pretending that she is first the sun and then the moon. She's actually speaking in the voices of the sun and the moon. Listen carefully; what does she tell us? Can't you just picture yourself up in the sky as the sun and the moon?

You're going to be writing your own poems where you pretend that you're something in nature. I'd like you to choose something large from nature that you could pretend to be: the sun, the moon, a tree, the ocean, a cloud, . . . and I'd like you to close your eyes, and pretend that you are that. Tell the person next to you what thing in nature you are.

Now, keep pretending you're that thing in nature. Think of four words that describe yourself, and turn to someone next to you and tell them those four words. You might want to begin your poems with those words.

Think now of what you do as the sun or the ocean. What do you do best? If you're the sun, for example, what do you do best? Light up the world? Keep children warm? Share with the person next to you what things you do best for the world.

Extensions

- Give each child a blank paper plate with holes cut out for eyes, so children can create a mask to help them become whatever they are pretending to be in their poem. When they say or read their poems, they can put their paper-plate masks up to their faces.
- Children can leave off the titles of their personification poems when they read them, so that other children can guess what they are.

Book Links

These books can help you extend the minilesson.

Rebecca Kai Dotlich
When Riddles Come Rumbling: Poems to Ponder
Boyds Mills Press (2001)

Douglas Florian
Lizards, Frogs, and Polliwogs
Harcourt (2001)

Jane Yolen
Once Upon Ice: And Other Frozen Poems
Boyds Mills Press (1997). See "Proteus" by Christine Crow.

Paul Janeczko
Dirty Laundry Pile: Poems in Different Voices
HarperCollins (2001)

Letter Poems

Anything in life that you care about is worth keeping,
maybe in a poem. —X. J. Kennedy

A letter poem, or apostrophe poem, is a poem of direct address—a kind of letter to someone or something. Letter poems work well if children want to speak to someone who is not present or speak to something that is missing. Children can also use this form if they just want to appreciate something or someone they love.

Minilesson

Today I'd like to read a poem by Jane Yolen. She does something very interesting in her poem "Puppy Love" (*Climb Inside a Poem* big book, p. 21). The poet speaks to the puppy that she sees in the window. She doesn't say, "I see a puppy in the window." She speaks to him, "Oh, puppy. . . ." This kind of poem is a little like a letter. There's a fancy word for this kind of poem; it's called an "apostrophe poem." Here, let me write that for you to see. A letter or apostrophe poem is when you speak to someone or something in your poem. You could speak to a puppy, a firefly, your grandmother, the moon, really anything.

Now the key to this kind of poem is not just to say, "Hi, firefly, how are you? My name is ____." The key is to describe the firefly. What would you really want to say to a firefly or a puppy?

I'll read to you two more examples, "Dear Friend in the Desert" by Kristine O'Connell George and "Hey, Crow!" by Deborah Chandra (*Climb Inside a Poem* big book, p. 6, p. 33).

Now you try!

Book Links

These poems in the *Climb Inside a Poem* big book are letter poems:

"Dear Friend in the Desert" by Kristine O'Connell George p. 6

"Hey Crow!" by Deborah Chandra p. 33

"Puppy Love" by Jane Yolen p. 21

These books can help you extend the minilesson.

Douglas Florian
Lizards, Frogs, and Polliwogs
Harcourt (2001). See "The Python" and "The Chameleon."

Douglas Florian
Mammalabilia
Harcourt (2000). See "The Bactrian Camel."

Douglas Florian
Insectlopedia
Harcourt (1998). See "The Daddy Longlegs."

Eloise Greenfield
In the Land of Words: New and Selected Poems
Amistad (2004). See "Poem."

Lee Bennett Hopkins
Got Geography
Greenwillow (2006). See "The Mountain" by David Harrison and "Compass" by Maria Fleming.

Jane Yolen
Once Upon Ice: And Other Frozen Poems
Boyds Mills Press (1997). See "Pyramid" by Shulamith Levey Oppenheim.

Paul Janeczko
Hey You: Poems to Skyscrapers, Mosquitoes, and Other Fun Things
HarperCollins (2007)

SECTION 4
Revision

As the brown bat in *The Bat-Poet* by Randall Jarrell (HarperCollins 1997) says after sharing his poems: "The trouble isn't finding someone who will hear the poems. The trouble is finding someone who will truly listen."

Listening is the key to teaching children to write poetry well. Guiding students by listening to their poems, and by helping them listen to their own poems, is the core of revising.

Three Essential Ways to Help Children Revise Their Poems

Let go. Celebrate this poem with the child and use her new confidence to support her revision the next time around.

After listening to a poem read aloud by the poet, say that you'd like to read it back. Ask the poet to listen carefully while you read. After reading the poem out loud, ask, "What did you notice about your poem?" Or ask, "What do you think about your poem?"

When poets say, "I like it," or "I think it's great," celebrate their confidence and belief in themselves. Ask them to tell you one part that they particularly liked. Then celebrate and affirm one thing you think that the poet has done well. For example, you might point out:

- I like the way you wrote about something that matters to you—the poem was written from your heart.
- I like the way that your poem has a beat to it—it's like a little song. Can we tap our fingers on the table to the rhythm of it?
- I like the way you repeated a few words. Poets use repetition a lot in their poems, just like you did.
- I like how you chose to write about something that you knew a lot about.
- I like the words you used—that's a brand new way of describing ____.
- Your drawing has so many details in it.
- I like the way you got started writing right away.

On some occasions, it's better for the student to celebrate than to revise!

Asking questions can always be helpful in revising a poem.

The second conference strategy is to ask a question to guide poets in developing or revising a poem. These questions are helpful:

- Are there any other mind-pictures that you saw in your mind as I read the poem? Where might you like to add those?
- Listen to your poem—how does it sound? Is there anything you think you need to change or add?
- I'd like you to listen to the ending of your poem, and tell me what you notice.
- I'm going to read your poem back to you, and I'd like you to tell me: does it sound like a poem or more like a story?

Speak to the poet's ways of writing, not the specific poem.

Since young poets tend to finish their poems quickly, conferences should involve more than one poem. Ask a poet to spread out on the desk all the poems that he or she has written, so you can see them all at once. Read them quickly to yourself, and try to see a pattern in the poems. Find one treasure, and give a compliment on one thing the poet has done well. Find one area where you can help guide a young poet in revising.

The preceding general guidelines may help you. What follows are some specific revision lessons that make a positive difference.

Adding Stanzas

[Revision] is like polishing a rough stone and finding that it has become a glittering diamond. —Joseph Bruchac

[When you revise,] cross out [parts] and start over and doodle and make lists of possible words and circle things and draw arrows all over the place indicating places to move or insert lines. —Alice Schertle

Young poets tend to write a few words and then say, "I'm finished!" Or they may write a big "THE END" at the bottom of their papers. Showing them that poems sometimes have two or three stanzas helps young poets to develop their poems further. Young poets can add another stanza that day, or over several days. To prepare for this minilesson, you'll need to make a chart-paper copy of "Happy Toes" by Pat Mora (*Climb Inside a Poem* big book, p. 5) or "Sky Wish" by Rebecca Kai Dotlich (*Climb Inside a Poem* big book, p. 4). Tape a piece of blank paper over the second and third stanzas, leaving only the first stanza visible.

Minilesson

Poets, I want to talk to you about something that poets do when they think they're finished their poems. Sometimes we write a few words and think, "I'm finished with my poem!" But look at this poem, "Happy Toes" by Pat Mora, on this chart paper. I'll read the first part. Now, this poet could have stopped here and said, "I'm done with my poem!" Instead, she closed her eyes and thought a little more about her poem and realized that she had more to say. So, she skipped a big space and then added this next part, which I'll read to you.

I'd like you to return to your seats, and when you're writing your poems today, take another piece of paper and tape it onto your poem to add a few more words.

Listening Carefully

It's hard, also, having only yourself to judge your own work. Is it good? Is it the best I can do?

—Rebecca Kai Dotlich

When you re-read your poem, make changes until the taste, meaning, and sound of your words makes you feel like saying, "Yes! That's what I want to say."

—Bobbi Katz

Speaking our poems out loud as we write them, rereading a piece of writing as we're writing and after we're finished, becomes a way to practice reading and clarifying our poems. The minilesson demonstrates this strategy with one student in front of the class. To get ready for this minilesson, set up two chairs, and ask a young poet to bring her or his poem and sit in one chair, while you sit in the other chair.

Minilesson

Today I'm going to show you something that poets do all the time. While writing, poets reread their poems every time they add something new. After poets finish writing a poem, they ask a friend to read it back to them, or poets can read a poem aloud to themselves. Hearing your poem read by someone else can help you listen to see if there is anything to change or add to your poems. I'd like one of you to come sit beside me, in this chair.

Now, I'm going to read your poem back to you, and I'll ask you to close your eyes while I read. As I'm reading, think if there is anything you to want to add to your poem. Here we go!

If there is something you want to add, grab a pencil and change it right here! Great!

When you're finished with your poems, quietly read them back to yourselves first. Then look around to see who else in the class looks like they are ready to listen to your poem. See what changes you want to make to your poems after you hear them.

Ending Lines: "Don't leave the door wide open!"

Any serious writer . . . has a "dream" version that she or he is trying to achieve. —Pat Mora

Endings are tricky for all writers, not just poets. Young writers are tempted to write "THE END" in large letters to indicate that a story or poem is finished. We can help them reach for more complicated, more satisfying, more powerful conclusions for their writing. This minilesson on ending lines will help young poets find and create strong endings for their poems.

Minilesson

Today I want to talk to you about ways poets find endings for their poems. The ending is very important because it's the last thing that the reader reads in the poem. Without an ending, it's like walking out of your house, and leaving the door wide open!

Here are three different ways you might try to write an ending line for your poems:

One way is to choose a word or line that you think is really good or important, and make that your end line. Let's find an example in our *Climb Inside a Poem* big book. Listen to "Where Do I Find Poetry?" by Georgia Heard (pp. 2–3). Why do you think the poet chose that line for her end line? "Happy Toes" by Pat Mora (p. 5) ends with just three words. Why is that a good end line?

The second way to end your poem is to repeat the poem's first line. That makes a kind of a "sandwich poem" with the same beginning and ending. Can you think of an example? We don't have an example in our big book, but Langston Hughes did that in a poem called, simply, "Poem." His first line was, "I loved my friend" and then he repeated it for his last line, "I loved my friend."

The third way to end your poem is to write how you *feel*. If your poem is about your dog, it might end "And I love my dog." If your poem is about stars, it might end "The stars make me feel magical." Langston Hughes did that, too, in a different poem, "April Rain Song." In the last line, he shares how he feels: "And I love the rain." In our big book, "School Bus Lady" by J. Patrick Lewis (p. 15), "Poem for My Friend" by Patricia Hubbell (p. 16), and "Best Friend" by Marilyn Singer (p. 17) end with how the poet feels.

There are many other ways to end your poems, and you may want to invent your own way. When you're writing today, think about how you want to end your poems.

Book Links

These books can help you extend the minilesson.

Langston Hughes
The Dream Keeper and Other Poems
Knopf (1996)

Frank Asch
Just Like Daddy
Simon & Schuster (1981)

Jules Feiffer
Bark, George
Laura Geringer (1999)

Barbara Abercrombie
Charlie Anderson
Margaret K. McElderry (1990)

Richard Waring
Hungry Hen
HarperCollins (2001)

Jack Prelutsky
The 20th Century Children's Poetry Treasury
Knopf (1999)

Titles: Labels and Beyond

Tap your own creative energy and believe, really believe,
that you can write the poem that no one else can.
Your poem. Yours. —Rebecca Kai Dotlich

As part of the poetry writing unit, I point out that all poems have titles, and before a poem can be finished young poets need to write a title for their poems. I also suggest that they title their poems after they finish writing the poem, and not first thing.

For most young poets, their titles will be labels. For example, if a poem is about a dog, they might title it "Dog" or "My Dog." This is certainly the easiest way to title a poem, and a strategy that a lot of grown-up poets use a lot too. For poets who are ready, you can give an extension minilesson on other ways they might title their poems.

Minilesson

I want to point out something that all poems must have before they can be considered finished, and that's a title. The easiest time to title a poem is after you finish writing your poem. The reason why most poets title their poems after they finish writing them is that we don't know everything that's going to be in our poem until we're finished writing it, and if we start with a title, it limits what we might write about.

After you finish writing your poem, brainstorm a few titles for your poem before you choose the one you'll use. Let's say you're writing a poem about eating pizza. What title could we give the poem? Pizza? That would be the easiest—then everyone would know what the poem is about. But we could also brainstorm other ideas. Does anyone have other ideas for titles for a poem about pizza—maybe a title that might be a little different?

Extensions

Here are some more strategies poets use to title their poems, with examples from the *Climb Inside a Poem* big book:

- Take an important line or word from the poem and make that the title ("Singing Down the Sun" by Marilyn Singer, p. 32)

- Summarize the feeling or experience of the poem in the title ("Happy Toes" by Pat Mora, p. 5, and "When I Ride My Bike" by Patricia Hubbell, p. 14)
- Create a surprise title ("Spring Riddles" by Beverly McLoughland, p. 29, and "Hidden Treasure" by Bobbi Katz, p. 34)
- Make the title the first line of the poem ("Dear Friend in the Desert" by Kristine O'Connell George, p. 6)

Book Links

This book can help you extend the minilesson.

Beverly McLoughland
A Hippo's a Heap: And Other Animal Poems
Boyds Mills Press (1993)

Reflecting and Celebrating

Reflection and Self-Assessment

Every poet stands back and reflects on the work he or she has written, both as a way to move her or his poems forward and to celebrate good work already done. Children can periodically assess and reflect on their process and experience of poetry writing throughout the poetry workshop, not just at the end. Reflection can be done either orally or by writing and then discussing. Here are some questions that can prompt a discussion:

- What is your favorite poem you've written so far? Why?
- What do you do really well in your poetry writing?
- What are two things you've learned about writing poetry that you didn't know before?
- What writing advice would you give children just your age who are just learning to write poems?
- What do you think we should add to the What We Know About Poetry chart?

Celebrations: Sharing Poems Beyond Our Walls

You and your children will be eager to share their writing as you draw the poetry unit to an end. A poetry celebration is wonderful way to bring closure to the study. There are many ways to celebrate children's new insights about poems and poets, their new confidence as readers of poetry, and their new competence as writers of poetry. Here are a few possibilities:

• Class Poetry Reading and Anthology

Periodically (you don't have to wait until the end of the poetry writing unit), ask poets to select their favorite or best poem that they've written so far. Ask them to practice reading it to a friend. They can put those poems aside for later publication.

At the end of the poetry writing unit, each poet can choose a favorite poem to share at a class poetry reading. It's helpful to bring in a portable microphone to help young poets hear all the poems. To make it a special day, they can salute each other with apple juice and recite a favorite poem together. You might invite in another class as well. After the reading, collect your students' poems to share in a class anthology. Ask a parent or an older student to help type their poems using big print, and publish their original words and drawings next to the published big print version.

• Posting Poems Around the School

Remind your young poets that you already have poems posted around the room. Perhaps you have a poem by the pencil sharpener, a poem about washing hands by the sink, and a poem about time posted next to the clock. Those poems are reminders that poets can write about anything. Those poems help us to remember that poetry is all around us, waiting for us to notice and gather ideas as we write our own poems. For this celebration, you and your young poets will identify places in the school where people usually gather and often must wait in line. Invite children to write poems about some of these places, and "publish" them there as well. Those include such places as:

- Water fountains
- Around the restroom doors
- Entrance to the library
- Entrance to the gym
- Entrance to the cafeteria
- Cafeteria serving line
- Cafeteria line for returning trays
- School office
- Nurse's office
- Teacher workroom

For these presentations, print the poems in a large, clear font that will be easily read by those waiting in line. Then mount them on large sheets of construction paper that will serve as a mat or frame. Your young poets may wish to decorate the edges. These may be laminated to make them more durable. Display poetry posters in the designated spots where they can be read by everyone in the school.

• Milk and Cookies "Coffee House"

Create a coffee house atmosphere in the classroom. Bring in lamps, close the blinds, and turn off the overhead lights. Create a cozy corner with a floor lamp that can "spotlight" the featured poet. Using blue "painter's tape," make a square on the floor to mark a special spot for the poet to stand. If it is possible, have a microphone for the poet. Poets can sign up for a time to present a favorite poem from their own writing. The audience will be seated at tables with little plates of cookies and cups of milk to enjoy as they listen to poets presenting their work. As is the tradition at a poetry reading, the audience will snap (as opposed to clapping) to show appreciation of the poet's work. To close the coffee house, have each poet sign a banner that will be hung in the "poet's corner," and place it there with an anthology of all the work read.

- **Poetry Luncheon**

There are at least two ways to host a poetry luncheon. One is to follow the model of the "Coffee House," and have lunch served in the classroom that day. The other is to schedule the poetry presentations during the lunchtime of other classes in the grade level or span. Arrange for a microphone (or microphones) to be set up in the cafeteria, and create a schedule of poets to present. The poets may choose to work in teams of two to four; and they may present poems they have selected from their own work or from your anthologies, the mentor texts I've included, or the poems in the big book. Since this audience will be larger, it may be more comfortable for your young poets to work in teams and to use poems they have lived with over time. As they plan for the presentations, encourage them to tap into the ways they have climbed inside poetry throughout the year.

- **Poetry Presents**

Each poet will select one person in the school or from home to gift with a poem. The selected poem will be printed on "fancy" paper and placed in a folder to be decorated by the poet. On a designated day—Poetry Presence/Presents Day—each poet will present his or her recipient with the Poetry Present, making the Presence of Poetry visible throughout the school.

- **Poetry Presentations**

Organize your young poets into teams of two to four, and schedule each team to present their poems as a read aloud for other classes. The poets will need to select one poem each from what they have written, and then decide how to present it. They may read it alone in one voice, or have the other team members contribute their voices as well. The poet may decide to read the poem and have the team members snap, clap, or pat a rhythm or use rhythm instruments. Some poets may choose to involve the audience, or to present the poem with hand gestures or some dramatic movements.

- **Poetry Gallery**

Display each child's poem inside a white paper frame to create a poetry gallery, and include their illustrations as well. Or you can purchase small Plexiglas frames to display their poems in the gallery.

- **Poetry Cards**

Children can select one of their written poems to be laminated as a poetry card. The poetry cards may be kept in a basket near the poetry books for others to read.

- **Listening Tapes**

Children can each select one of their favorite written poems and practice reading it aloud. The class can then create a taped anthology of poems to accompany their printed poetry anthology.

Conclusion

However you choose to celebrate with your students about their new knowledge and the changes in them as developing poets, be sure you do celebrate! Make sure to celebrate your own teaching work as well, whether you do it privately or with colleagues. After all, what you have done is not small. You've brought the art and power of poetry to your part of a generation of young children just as they are peeping into the wider world, just as they are forming their opinions of what matters and of how the world can be. And that teaching, that offering you've given, is deeply worthy of celebration.

Bibliography

Abercrombie, Barbara. 1990. *Charlie Anderson*. New York: Margaret K. McElderry.

Adams, Diane. 2005. *Zoom!* Atlanta: Peachtree.

Adoff, Arnold. 2000. *Touch The Poem*. New York: Blue Sky Press.

Asch, Frank. 1981. *Just Like Daddy*. New York: Simon & Schuster.

Bauer, Marion Dane. 1996. *When I Go Camping with Grandma*. Mahwah, NJ: Bridgewater Books.

Baylor, Byrd. 1978. *The Other Way to Listen*. New York: Atheneum.

Baylor, Byrd. 1978. *The Way to Start a Day*. New York: Atheneum.

Behn, Harry. 1994. *Trees*. New York: Henry Holt.

Brown, Marc. 1985. *Hand Rhymes*. New York: Dutton.

Brown, Margaret Wise. 1994. *Four Fur Feet*. New York: Hyperion.

Brown, Margaret Wise. 2007 edition. *Nibble Nibble*. New York: HarperCollins.

Browne, Michael Dennis. 2004. *Give Her the River: A Father's Wish for His Daughter*. New York: Atheneum.

Bruchac, Joseph and Jonathan London. 1992. *Thirteen Moons on Turtle's Back: A Native American Year of Moons*. New York: Philomel.

Bruchac, Joseph. 1995. *The Earth Under Sky Bear's Feet*. New York: Philomel.

Bruchac, Joseph. 1999. *Between Earth and Sky: Legends of Native American Sacred Places*. New York: Voyager Books.

Bruchac, Joseph. 2002. *Seasons of the Circle: A Native American Year*. Mahwah, NJ: Troll.

Bruchac, Joseph. 2004. *Many Nations: An Alphabet of Native America*. New York: Scholastic.

Carle, Eric. 1993. *Today is Monday*. New York: Philomel.

Chandra, Deborah. 1994. *Miss Mabel's Table*. San Diego: Harcourt.

Chandra, Deborah. 1995. *Who Comes?* San Francisco: Sierra Club Books for Children.

Chandra, Deborah. 1996. *Rich Lizard: And Other Poems*. New York: Sunburst.

Chandra, Deborah. 1999. *A Is for Amos*. New York: Farrar, Straus and Giroux.

Chandra, Deborah. 2003. *George Washington's Teeth*. New York: Farrar, Straus and Giroux.

Chandra, Deborah. 2006. *Balloons: And Other Poems*. New York: Farrar, Straus and Giroux.

Cooper, Elisha. 2006. *Beach*. New York: Orchard Books.

Creech, Sharon. 2002. *Love That Dog* (audiobook). New York: HarperChildren's Audio.

Currey, Anna. 1999. *I Want Another Little Brother: Poems About Families*. New York: Penguin.

Degan, Bruce. 1996. *Jamberry* (audio cassette). New York: HarperCollins.

Dillon, Leo and Diane Dillon. 2002. *Rap A Tap Tap: Here's Bojangles—Think of That!* New York: Blue Sky Press.

Dotlich, Rebecca Kai. 1998. *Lemonade Sun: And Other Summer Poems*. Honesdale, PA: Boyds Mills Press.

Dotlich, Rebecca Kai. 2000. *Sweet Dreams of the Wild: Poems for Bedtime*. Honesdale, PA: Boyds Mills Press.

Dotlich, Rebecca Kai. 2001. *When Riddles Come Rumbling: Poems to Ponder*. Honesdale, PA: Boyds Mills Press.

Dotlich, Rebecca Kai. 2003. *In the Spin of Things: Poetry of Motion*. Honesdale, PA: Boyds Mills Press.

Dotlich, Rebecca Kai. 2004. *Over in the Pink House: New Jump-Rope Rhymes*. Honesdale, PA: Boyds Mills Press.

Dotlich, Rebecca Kai. 2006. *What Is Science?* New York: Henry Holt.

Edwards, Pamela Duncan. 1996. *Some Smug Slug*. New York: HarperCollins.

Engelbreit, Mary. 2008. *Mary Engelbreit's Mother Goose Book and CD*. New York: HarperCollins; Har/Com.

Esbensen, Barbara Juster. 1998. *Words with Wrinkled Knees: Animal Poems*. Honesdale, PA: Boyds Mills Press.

Esbensen, Barbara Juster. 2002. *Swing Around the Sun: Poems*. Minneapolis, MN: Lerner.

Feiffer, Jules. 1999. *Bark, George*. New York: Laura Geringer.

Fisher, Aileen. 1991. *Always Wondering: Some Favorite Poems of Aileen Fisher*. New York: HarperCollins.

Fisher, Aileen. 2005. *Know What I Saw*. Brookfield, CT: Roaring Brook Press.

Fisher, Valorie. 2003. *Ellsworth's Extraordinary Electric Ears and Other Amazing Alphabet Anecdotes*. New York: Atheneum.

Fitch, Sheree. 2001. *No Two Snowflakes*. Custer, WA: Orca Book Publishers.

Fleischman, Paul. 1988. *Joyful Noise: Poems for Two Voices*. New York: Laura Geringer.

Fleischman, Paul. 1989. *I Am Phoenix: Poems for Two Voices*. New York: HarperTrophy.

Fleischman, Paul. 2001. *Joyful Noise/I Am Phoenix* (audio cassette). Middletown, RI: Audio Bookshelf.

Fletcher, Ralph. 1997. *Ordinary Things: Poems from a Walk in Early Spring*. New York: Atheneum.

Fletcher, Ralph. 1997. *Twilight Comes Twice*. New York: Clarion.

Fletcher, Ralph. 2003. *Hello, Harvest Moon*. New York: Clarion.

Fletcher, Ralph. 2005. *A Writing Kind of Day: Poems for Young Poets*. Honesdale, PA: Boyds Mills Press.

Florian, Douglas. 1998. *Insectlopedia*. San Diego: Harcourt.

Florian, Douglas. 2000. *Mammalabilia*. San Diego: Harcourt.

Florian, Douglas. 2001. *Lizards, Frogs, and Polliwogs*. San Diego: Harcourt.

Florian, Douglas. 2006. *Handsprings*. New York: Greenwillow.

Florian, Douglas. 2007. *Comets, Stars, the Moon, and Mars: Space Poems and Paintings*. San Diego: Harcourt.

Fox, Mem. 1993. *Time for Bed*. San Diego: Gulliver.

Fox, Mem. 1994. *Koala Lou*. New York: Voyager Books.

Fox, Mem. 1997. *Whoever You Are*. San Diego: Harcourt.

Fox, Mem. 2002. *The Magic Hat*. San Diego: Harcourt.

George, Kristine O'Connell. 1999. *Little Dog Poems*. New York: Clarion.

George, Kristine O'Connell. 2001. *Toasting Marshmallows: Camping Poems*. New York: Clarion.

George, Kristine O'Connell. 2002. *Little Dog and Duncan*. New York: Clarion.

George, Kristine O'Connell. 2004. *Hummingbird Nest: A Journal of Poems*. San Diego: Harcourt.

George, Kristine O'Connell. 2005. *Fold Me a Poem*. San Diego: Harcourt.

George, Kristine O'Connell. 2005. *The Great Frog Race: And Other Poems*. New York: Clarion.

George, Kristine O'Connell. 2005. *Up!* New York: Clarion.

George, Kristine O'Connell. 2007. *Old Elm Speaks: Tree Poems*. New York: Clarion.

Giovanni, Nikki. 1987. *Spin a Soft Black Song: Poems for Children*. New York: Farrar, Straus and Giroux.

Gollub, Matthew. 1998. *Cool Melons—Turn to Frogs!: The Life and Poems of Issa*. New York: Lee & Low Books.

Graves, Donald. 1996. *Baseball, Snakes, and Summer Squash: Poems About Growing Up*. Honesdale, PA: Boyds Mills Press.

Greenburg, Jan. 2001. *Heart to Heart: New Poems Inspired by Twentieth-Century American Art*. New York: Harry N. Abrams.

Greenfield, Eloise. 1986. *Honey, I Love and Other Love Poems*. New York: HarperTrophy.

Greenfield, Eloise. 2004. *In the Land of Words: New and Selected Poems*. New York: Amistad.

Greenfield, Eloise. 2006. *The Friendly Four*. New York: Amistad.

Griego, Margot C. and Betsy L. Bucks, Sharon S. Gilbert, and Laurel H. Kimball. 1981. *Tortillas Para Mamá: And Other Nursery Rhymes/Spanish and English*. New York: Henry Holt.

Grimes, Nikki. 2000. *Shoe Magic*. New York: Scholastic.

Grimes, Nikki. 2006. *Thanks a Million*. New York: Amistad.

Grimes, Nikki. 2006. *Welcome, Precious*. New York: Orchard Books.

Harrison, David L. 1999. *Wild Country: Outdoor Poems for Young People*. Honesdale, PA: Boyds Mills Press.

Harrison, David L. 2000. *Farmer's Garden: Rhymes for Two Voices*. Honesdale, PA: Boyds Mills Press.

Harrison, David L. 2003. *The Mouse Was Out at Recess*. Honesdale, PA: Boyds Mills Press.

Harrison, David L. 2005. *Farmer's Dog Goes to the Forest: Rhymes for Two Voices*. Honesdale, PA: Boyds Mills Press.

Heard, Georgia. 1997. *Creatures of Earth, Sea, and Sky*. Honesdale, PA: Boyds Mills Press.

Heard, Georgia. 2000. *Songs of Myself: An Anthology of Poems and Art*. New York: Mondo.

Heard, Georgia. 2002, reissued 2006. *This Place I Know: Poems of Comfort*. Cambridge, MA: Candlewick.

Heard, Georgia. 2008. *Falling Down the Page: List Poems*. Brookfield, CT: Roaring Brook Press.

Henkes, Kevin. 2003. *All Alone*. NY: New York: Greenwillow.

Hittleman, Carol G. and Daniel R. Hittleman. 2002. *A Grand Celebration: Grandparents in Poetry*. Honesdale, PA: Boyds Mills Press.

Hoban, Tana. 1986. *Shapes, Shapes, Shapes*. New York: Greenwillow.

Hoban, Tana. 1987. *Dots, Spots, Speckles, and Stripes*. New York: Greenwillow.

Hoban, Tana. 1988. *Look! Look! Look!* New York: Greenwillow.

Hoberman, Mary Ann. 2001. *You Read to Me, I'll Read to You: Very Short Stories to Read Together*. New York: Little, Brown.

Hopkins, Lee Bennett. 1986. *Best Friends*. New York: HarperCollins.

Hopkins, Lee Bennett. 1988. *Side by Side: Poems to Read Together*. New York: Simon & Schuster.

Hopkins, Lee Bennett. 1990. *Good Books, Good Times!* New York: Harper & Row.

Hopkins, Lee Bennett. 1994. *Questions: Poems (I Can Read)*. New York: HarperTrophy.

Hopkins, Lee Bennett. 1995. *Been to Yesterdays: Poems of a Life*. Honesdale, PA: Boyds Mills Press.

Hopkins, Lee Bennett. 1996. *School Supplies: A Book of Poems.* New York: Simon & Schuster.

Hopkins, Lee Bennett. 1999. *Lives: Poems About Famous Americans.* New York: HarperCollins.

Hopkins, Lee Bennett. 1999. *Sports! Sports! Sports! A Poetry Collection.* New York: HarperCollins.

Hopkins, Lee Bennett. 2000. *Happy Birthday.* New York: Simon & Schuster.

Hopkins, Lee Bennett. 2002 reprint. *Spectacular Science: A Book of Poems.* New York: Aladdin.

Hopkins, Lee Bennett. 2003. *Alphathoughts: Alphabet Poems.* Honesdale, PA: Boyds Mills Press.

Hopkins, Lee Bennett. 2004. *Days to Celebrate: A Full Year of Poetry, People, Holidays, History, Fascinating Facts, and More.* New York: Greenwillow.

Hopkins, Lee Bennett. 2004. *Home to Me: Poems Across America.* New York: Scholastic.

Hopkins, Lee Bennett. 2004. *Wonderful Words: Poems About Reading, Writing, Speaking, and Listening.* New York: Simon & Schuster.

Hopkins, Lee Bennett. 2006. *Got Geography!* New York: Greenwillow.

Hopkins, Lee Bennett. 2007. *Behind the Museum Door: Poems to Celebrate the Wonders of Museums.* New York: Abrams Books for Young Readers.

Hopkins, Lee Bennett.1992. *Flit, Flutter, Fly: Poems About Bugs and Other Crawly Creatures.* New York: Doubleday.

Hubbell, Patricia. 2000. *Earthmates: Poems.* New York: Cavendish.

Hubbell, Patricia. 2001. *Black Earth, Gold Sun.* New York: Cavendish.

Hubbell, Patricia. 2001. *City Kids: Poems.* New York: Cavendish.

Hubbell, Patricia. 2002. *Rabbit Moon: A Book of Holidays and Celebrations.* New York: Cavendish.

Hubbell, Patricia. 2003. *Black All Around!* New York: Lee & Low Books.

Hubbell, Patricia. 2005. *Hurray for Spring!* New York: Cavendish.

Hubbell, Patricia. 2005. *Trains: Steaming! Pulling! Huffing!* New York: Cavendish.

Huck, Charlotte. 1993. *Secret Places.* New York: Greenwillow.

Hughes, Langston. 1996. *The Dream Keeper and Other Poems.* New York: Knopf.

Janeczko, Paul. 1990. *The Place My Words Are Looking For: What Poets Say About and Through Their Work.* New York: Simon & Schuster.

Janeczko, Paul. 2001. *Dirty Laundry Pile: Poems in Different Voices.* New York: HarperCollins.

Janeczko, Paul. 2002. *Seeing the Blue Between: Advice and Inspiration for Young Poets.* Cambridge, MA: Candlewick.

Janeczko, Paul. 2007. *Hey, You!: Poems to Skyscrapers, Mosquitoes, and Other Fun Things.* New York: HarperCollins.

Johnston, Tony. 2000. *The Barn Owls.* Watertown, MA: Charlesbridge.

Katz, Bobbi. 1996. *Germs, Germs, Germs!* New York: Scholastic.

Katz, Bobbi. 1997. *Could We Be Friends? Poems for Pals.* New York: Mondo.

Katz, Bobbi. 1997. *Truck Talk: Rhymes on Wheels.* New York: Scholastic.

Katz, Bobbi. 1999. *Make Way for Tooth Decay.* New York: Scholastic.

Katz, Bobbi. 2001. *A Rumpus of Rhymes: A Book of Noisy Poems.* New York: Dutton.

Katz, Bobbi. 2004. *Pocket Poems.* New York: Dutton.

Katz, Bobbi. 2006. *Once Around the Sun.* San Diego: Harcourt.

Katz, Bobbi. 2007. *Partner Poems for Building Fluency.* New York: Scholastic.

Katz, Bobbi. 2007. *Trailblazers: Poems of Exploration.* New York: Greenwillow.

Katz, Bobbi. 2008. *More Pocket Poems.* New York: Dutton.

Kelly, Irene. 2007. *It's a Butterfly's Life.* New York: Holiday House.

Kennedy, X. J. 1985. *The Forgetful Wishing Well: Poems for Young People.* New York: Atheneum.

Kennedy, X. J. 1986. *Brats.* New York: Margaret K. McElderry.

Kennedy, X. J. 1991. *The Kite That Braved Old Orchard Beach: Year-Round Poems for Young People.* New York: Margaret K. McElderry.

Kennedy, X. J. 1992. *The Beasts of Bethlehem.* New York: Margaret K. McElderry.

Kennedy, X. J. 1999 rev. ed. *Knock at a Star: A Child's Introduction to Poetry.* New York: Little, Brown.

Kennedy, X. J. 1999. *Elympics: Poems.* New York: Philomel.

Kennedy, X. J. 2002. *Exploding Gravy: Poems to Make You Laugh.* New York: Little, Brown.

Kennedy, X. J. and Dorothy Kennedy. 1992. *Talking Like the Rain: A Read-to-Me Book of Poems.* New York: Little, Brown.

Kuskin, Karla. 1975. *Near the Window Tree: Poems and Notes.* New York: HarperCollins.

Kuskin, Karla. 2003. *Moon, Have You Met My Mother?* New York: HarperCollins.

Kuskin, Karla. 2004. *Roar and More.* Honesdale, PA: Boyds Mills Press.

Laminack, Lester L. 2004. *Saturdays and Teacakes.* Atlanta: Peachtree.

Leedy, Loreen. 2003. *There's a Frog in My Throat: 440 Animal Sayings a Little Bird Told Me*. New York: Holiday House.

Lewis, J. Patrick and Paul B. Janeczko. 2006. *Wing Nuts: Screwy Haiku*. New York: Little, Brown.

Lewis, J. Patrick. 2001. *Good Mousekeeping: And Other Animal Home Poems*. New York: Atheneum.

Lewis, J. Patrick. 2002. *A World of Wonders: Geographic Travels in Verse and Rhyme*. New York: Dial.

Lewis, J. Patrick. 2002. *Doodle Dandies: Poems That Take Shape*. New York: Aladdin.

Lewis, J. Patrick. 2003. *The Snowflake Sisters*. New York: Atheneum.

Lewis, J. Patrick. 2005. *God Made the Skunk: And Other Animal Poems*. Cupertino, CA: Doggerel Daze.

Lewis, J. Patrick. 2005. *Monumental Verses*. Washington, DC: National Geographic Children's Books.

Lewis, J. Patrick. 2005. *Please Bury Me in the Library*. San Diego: Gulliver.

Lewis, J. Patrick. 2006. *Good Mornin', Ms. America: The U.S.A. in Verse*. Greenville, WI: School Specialty.

Lewis, J. Patrick. 2007. *Big Is Big (and little, little): A Book of Contrasts*. New York: Holiday House.

Lewis, J. Patrick. 2007. *Tulip at the Bat*. New York: Little, Brown.

Lewis, J. Patrick. 2007. *Under the Kissletoe: Christmastime Poems*. Honesdale, PA: Boyds Mills Press.

Lillegard, Dee. 2006. *Go!: Poetry in Motion*. New York: Knopf.

Lindbergh, Reeve. 1993. *Grandfather's Lovesong*. New York: Viking.

Lindbergh, Reeve. 1997. *The Awful Aardvarks Go to School*. New York: Viking.

Lionni, Leo. 1967. *Frederick*. New York: Knopf.

Little, Jean. 1990. *Hey World, Here I Am!* New York: HarperTrophy.

Livingston, Myra Cohn. 2007. *Calendar*. New York: Holiday House.

Locker, Thomas. 1995. *Sky Tree: Seeing Science Through Art*. New York: HarperCollins.

Locker, Thomas. 1998. *Home: A Journey Through America*. San Diego: Silver Whistle.

Look, Lenore. 1999. *Love as Strong as Ginger*. New York: Atheneum.

MacLachlan, Patricia. 1994. *All the Places to Love*. New York: Joanna Cotler.

Martin, Bill, Jr. and John Archambault. 1989. *Chicka Chicka Boom Boom*. New York: Simon & Schuster.

McCord, David. 1999. *Every Time I Climb a Tree*. New York: Little, Brown.

McLoughland, Beverly. 1993. *A Hippo's a Heap: And Other Animal Poems*. Honesdale, PA: Boyds Mills Press.

McMillan, Bruce. 1988. *Fire Engine Shapes*. New York: Lothrop, Lee and Shepard.

Miller, David. 2001. *Just Like You and Me*. New York: Dial.

Moore, Lilian. 1976. *I Feel the Same Way*. New York: Atheneum.

Moore, Lilian. 2005. *Mural on Second Avenue and Other City Poems*. Cambridge, MA: Candlewick.

Mora, Pat. 1994. *Pablo's Tree*. New York: Simon & Schuster.

Mora, Pat. 1994. *The Desert Is My Mother: El Desierto Es Mi Madre*. Houston: Pinata.

Mora, Pat. 1996. *Uno, Dos, Tres: One, Two, Three*. New York: Clarion.

Mora, Pat. 1997 reprint ed. *A Birthday Basket For Tía*. New York: Aladdin.

Mora, Pat. 1997. *Tomás And the Library Lady*. New York: Knopf.

Mora, Pat. 2001 reprint ed. *Listen to the Desert: Oye al Desierto*. New York: Clarion.

Mora, Pat. 2001. *Love to Mamá: A Tribute to Mothers*. New York: Lee & Low Books.

Mora, Pat. 2001. *The Race of Toad And Deer*. Toronto: Groundwood.

Mora, Pat. 2005. *Doña Flor: A Tall Tale About A Giant Woman With A Great, Big Heart*. New York: Knopf.

Mora, Pat. 2006. *¡Marimba! Animales from A to Z*. New York: Clarion.

Mora, Pat. 2006. *Confetti: Poemas para Ninos / Poems For Children*. New York: Lee & Low.

Morrison, Lillian. 1992. *Whistling the Morning in*. Honesdale, PA: Boyds Mills Press.

Morrison, Lillian. 1997. *I Scream, You Scream: A Feast of Food Rhymes*. Atlanta: August House.

Myers, Walter Dean. 1993. *Brown Angels: An Album of Pictures and Verse*. New York: HarperCollins.

Paolilli, Paul and Dan Brewer. 2001. *Silver Seeds: A Book of Nature Poems*. New York: Viking.

Paschen, Elise, Dominique Raccah, Billy Collins, Nikki Giovanni, and X.J. Kennedy. 2005. *Poetry Speaks to Children* (Book and CD). Naperville, IL: Sourcebooks MediaFusion; Har/Com edition.

Philip, Neil. 2004. *Hot Potato: Mealtime Rhymes*. New York: Clarion

Prelutsky, Jack. 1983. *The Random House Book of Poetry for Children*. New York: Random House.

Prelutsky, Jack. 1986. *Read-Aloud Rhymes for the Very Young*. New York: Knopf.

Prelutsky, Jack. 1991. *For Laughing Out Loud: Poems to Tickle Your Funnybone.* New York: Knopf.

Prelutsky, Jack. 1999. *The 20th Century Children's Poetry Treasury.* New York: Knopf.

Prelutsky, Jack. 2004. *If Not for the Cat.* New York: Greenwillow.

Prelutsky, Jack. 2005. *Read a Rhyme, Write a Rhyme.* New York: Knopf.

Prelutsky, Jack. 2005. *The Jack Prelutsky Holiday CD Audio Collection.* New York: HarperChildren's Audio.

Rand, Ann and Paul Rand. 2006. *Sparkle and Spin: A Book About Words.* San Francisco: Chronicle Books.

Ross, Mandy. 2005. *Wake Up, Sleepy Head!: Early Morning Poems.* Wiltshire, U. K.: Child's Play International Ltd.

Rossetti, Christina. 1872. "Hurt No Living Thing." Available online. Also in *The Complete Poems* by Christina Rossetti, R. W. Crump, and Betty S. Flowers. New York: Penguin, 2001.

Rosten, Norman. 2004. *A City Is.* New York: Henry Holt.

Rotner, Shelley and Richard Olivo. 1997. *Close, Closer, Closest.* New York: Atheneum.

Rovetch, Lissa. 2001. *Ook the Book: And Other Silly Rhymes.* San Francisco: Chronicle.

Ryder, Joanne. 2006. *My Mother's Voice.* New York: HarperCollins.

Rylant, Cynthia. 1986. *Night in the Country.* New York: Atheneum/Richard Jackson Books.

Rylant, Cynthia. 2000. *In November.* San Diego: Harcourt.

Rylant, Cynthia. 2001. *Waiting to Waltz: A Childhood.* New York: Atheneum/Richard Jackson Books.

Schertle, Alice. 1997. *A Lucky Thing.* San Diego: Harcourt.

Schertle, Alice. 1998 reprint ed. *How Now, Brown Cow?* New York: Voyager.

Schertle, Alice. 2000 reprint ed. *Down The Road.* New York: Voyager Books.

Schertle, Alice. 2002. *All You Need For A Snowman.* New York: Scholastic.

Schertle, Alice. 2003. *¡Pió Peep!: Traditional Spanish Nursery Rhymes.* New York: HarperCollins.

Schertle, Alice. 2003. *Teddy Bear, Teddy Bear.* New York: HarperCollins.

Schertle, Alice. 2004. *1, 2, I Love You.* San Francisco: Chronicle Books.

Schertle, Alice. 2004. *All You Need For A Beach.* San Diego: Harcourt.

Schertle, Alice. 2006. *The Adventures of Old Bo Bear.* San Francisco: Chronicle.

Schertle, Alice. 2007. *Very Hairy Bear.* San Diego: Harcourt.

Schotter, Roni. 1999. *Nothing Ever Happens on 90th Street.* New York: Scholastic.

Schotter, Roni. 2006. *The Boy Who Loved Words.* New York: Random House.

Seabrooke, Brenda. 1995. *Looking for Diamonds.* New York: Dutton.

Seuling, Barbara. 2004. *Whose House?* San Diego: Gulliver.

Shannon, George. 2000. *Frog Legs: A Picture Book of Action Verse.* New York: Greenwillow.

Shannon, George. 2006. *Busy in the Garden.* New York: Greenwillow.

Shields, Carol Diggory. 1995. *Lunch Money: And Other Poems About School.* New York: Dutton.

Shields, Carol Diggory. 2003. *Almost Late to School: And More School Poems.* New York: Dutton.

Shulevitz, Uri. 1998. *Snow.* New York: Farrar, Straus and Giroux.

Sidman, Joyce. 2005. *Song of the Water Boatman & Other Pond Poems.* New York: Houghton Mifflin.

Silverstein, Shel. 2006. *Runny Babbit: A Billy Sook* (book and abridged CD). New York: HarperCollins; Har/Com.

Singer, Marilyn. 1993 reprint ed. *Nine O'Clock Lullaby.* New York: HarperTrophy.

Singer, Marilyn. 1994. *Sky Words.* New York: Macmillan.

Singer, Marilyn. 1997. *Chester the Out-of-Work Dog.* New York: Henry Holt.

Singer, Marilyn. 1998. *Good, Day, Good Night.* New York: Cavendish.

Singer, Marilyn. 2001 reprint ed. *On the Same Day in March: A Tour of the World's Weather.* New York: HarperTrophy.

Singer, Marilyn. 2002. *Quiet Night.* New York: Clarion.

Singer, Marilyn. 2003. *Fireflies at Midnight.* New York: Atheneum.

Singer, Marilyn. 2004. *Creature Carnival.* New York: Hyperion.

Spinelli, Eileen. 1998. *When Mama Comes Home Tonight.* New York: Simon & Schuster.

Spinelli, Eileen. 2004. *Feathers: Poems About Birds.* New York: Henry Holt.

Taberski, Sharon. 1996. *Morning, Noon, and Night: Poems to Fill Your Day.* New York: Mondo.

Thomas, Joyce Carol. 2002. *Crowning Glory.* New York: HarperCollins.

Waring, Richard. 2001. *Hungry Hen.* New York: HarperCollins.

Watson, Clyde. 2001. *Father Fox's Pennyrhymes.* New York: HarperCollins.

Weatherford, Carole Boston. 2001. *Sidewalk Chalk: Poems of the City*. Honesdale, PA: Boyds Mills Press.

Webb, Steve. 2004. *Tanka Tanka Skunk!* New York: Orchard Books.

Wild, Margaret. 1994. *Our Granny*. Boston: Houghton Mifflin.

Winer, Yvonne. 2002. *Birds Build Nests*. Watertown, MA: Charlesbridge.

Winters, Kay. 2001. *Did You See What I Saw?: Poems About School*. New York: Puffin.

Wong, Janet. 2000. *Night Garden: Poems from the World of Dreams*. New York: Margaret K. McElderry.

Wong, Janet. 2000. *The Trip Back Home*. San Diego: Harcourt.

Wong, Janet. 2000. *This Next New Year*. New York: Farrar, Straus and Giroux.

Wong, Janet. 2002 reprint ed. *Buzz*. New York: Voyager.

Wong, Janet. 2002. *Apple Pie 4th of July*. San Diego: Harcourt.

Wong, Janet. 2002. *You Have to Write*. New York: Margaret K. McElderry.

Wong, Janet. 2003. *Knock on Wood: Poems About Superstitions*. New York: Margaret K. McElderry.

Wong, Janet. 2003. *Minn and Jake*. New York: Farrar, Straus and Giroux.

Wong, Janet. 2007. *The Dumpster Diver*. Cambridge, MA: Candlewick.

Wong, Janet. 2007. *Twist: Yoga Poems*. New York: Margaret K. McElderry.

Worth, Valerie. 1994. *All the Small Poems and Fourteen More*. New York: Farrar, Straus and Giroux.

Worth, Valerie. 2002. *Peacock and Other Poems*. New York: Farrar, Straus and Giroux.

Yolen, Jane. 1987. *Owl Moon*. New York: Philomel.

Yolen, Jane. 1990. *Bird Watch*. New York: Philomel.

Yolen, Jane. 1995. *A Sip of Aesop*. New York: Scholastic.

Yolen, Jane. 1995. *Alphabestiary: Animal Poems from A to Z*. Honesdale, PA: Boyds Mills Press.

Yolen, Jane. 1996. *Sky Scrape / City Scape: Poems of City Life*. Honesdale, PA: Boyds Mills Press.

Yolen, Jane. 1997 reprint ed. *The Three Bears Rhyme Book*. San Diego: Harcourt.

Yolen, Jane. 1997. *Once Upon Ice: And Other Frozen Poems*. Honesdale, PA: Boyds Mills Press.

Yolen, Jane. 2000. *Color Me a Rhyme: Nature Poems for Young People*. Honesdale, PA: Boyds Mills Press.

Yolen, Jane. 2000. *How Do Dinosaurs Say Goodnight?* New York: Blue Sky Press.

Yolen, Jane. 2002. *Wild Wings: Poems for Young People*. Honesdale, PA: Boyds Mills Press.

Yolen, Jane. 2003. *Least Things: Poems About Small Natures*. Honesdale, PA: Boyds Mills Press.

Yolen, Jane. 2004. *Fine Feathered Friends: Poems for Young People*. Honesdale, PA: Boyds Mills Press.

Yolen, Jane. 2006. *Baby Bear's Books*. San Diego: Harcourt.

Yolen, Jane. 2006. *Count Me a Rhyme: Animal Poems by the Number*. Honesdale, PA: Wordsong.

Yolen, Jane. 2006. *Dimity Duck*. New York: Philomel.

Yolen, Jane. 2007. *Here's a Little Poem: A Very First Book of Poetry*. Cambridge, MA: Candlewick.

Young, Ed. 1992. *Seven Blind Mice*. New York: Philomel.

Bibliography of Poetry Websites and Blogs

Poetry Websites

Here are some favorite poetry websites where teachers can discover new poems, find favorites, and learn more about poetry:

Poets.org from the Academy of American Poets
http://www.poets.org/

Favorite Poem Project
http://www.favoritepoem.org/

Library of Congress Poetry Web page
http://www.loc.gov/poetry/

Library of Congress Poet Laureate Web page
http://www.loc.gov/poetry/laureate_current.html

National Schools Project Publishers of the Young American Poetry Digest
http://www.youngpoets.org/

A Choral Speaking Teacher's Guide
http://www.scriptsforschools.com/90.html

In addition to the poetry websites listed here, many of your favorite poets now have websites that will give you lots more material to share with your students.

Poetry Fridays Blogs

Dozens of blogs devoted to children's books celebrate "Poetry Fridays" by posting poems, reviewing poetry books, interviewing poets, and celebrating poetry in many ways. Here are a few blog addresses to get you started. (Warning: Be careful! You'll spend hours and hours at the computer!)

http://readingyear.blogspot.com

http://poetryforchildren.blogspot.com/

http://kidslitinformation.blogspot.com

http://chickenspaghetti.typepad.com/chicken_spaghetti